"A whirlwind of a biography . . . far stranger than fiction."

—*The Lady*

"A sophisticated, cultured cast of writers and thinkers are convincingly woven together through the fascination of the Paget twins, who are the magnetic centre of the story . . . *The Dazzling Paget Sisters* conjures a treasure trove of characters who were at the heart of their age."

—Virginia Nicholson

"A fascinating slice of social history seen through the lives of two dynamic, glamorous sisters. *The Dazzling Paget Sisters* also provides intriguing revelations about some of the great thinkers of the mid-twentieth century—George Orwell, Arthur Koestler, and Albert Camus—who were dazzled by the Paget twins. Hugely enjoyable."

—Julia Parry

"A work of art as well as a fount of tantalizing gossip."

—Michael Scammell

"*The Dazzling Paget Sisters* illuminates an intoxicating, almost lost world as never before, but its emotional heartbeat lies in the indissoluble trajectory of sibling love running through the lives of the magnetic Paget twins."

—Juliet Nicolson

"An irresistible family memoir by Ariane Bankes, the daughter of one of the Paget twins, identical and stunningly beautiful, who were born in 1916 and dazzled some of the most interesting men of the mid-twentieth century. In their entwined lives, George Orwell, Arthur Koestler, Albert Camus, A. J. Ayer and others played key parts, behaving more (Koestler) or less (Camus) badly: a gripping, tactfully told and moving story."

—Lucy Beckett,
Times Literary Supplement, Books of the Year 2024

"Identical twins Celia and Mamaine Paget are the focus of an engaging memoir by Celia's daughter, who draws on archival sources to create a warm, sensitive portrait of two extraordinary women . . . A captivating dual biography."

—*Kirkus Reviews*

"Oh, what lives they both led!"

—Anne de Courcy, *The Spectator*

THE DAZZLING
PAGET SISTERS

THE DAZZLING
PAGET SISTERS

THE ENGLISH TWINS
WHO CAPTIVATED LITERARY EUROPE

ARIANE BANKES

McNally Editions

New York

McNally Editions
134 Prince St.
New York, NY 10012

ISBN: 978-1-96134-135-7
E-book: 978-1-96134-136-4

Design by Jonathan Lippincott

1   3   5   7   9   10   8   6   4   2

CONTENTS

Mamaine and Celia Paget, photographed by Norman
Parkinson in October 1935 as 'The "Who's Who?" Pagets'

INTRODUCTION

What elusive quality is it that propels people into the centre of things? My mother, Celia Paget, and her identical twin sister Mamaine seemed to possess that quality, to gravitate towards the very heart of the era in which they lived. Born in 1916 and brought up in relative simplicity in rural Suffolk, their lives became entangled with some of the most remarkable figures of the twentieth century, whether as friends or lovers, muses or wives.

After my mother's death in 2002, I started to go through the contents of the old tin trunk she had left me. Yes, the proverbial trunk in the attic – so quaint, so nostalgic: today, its contents would all be scattered in the Cloud. But there it was, capacious and sooty black, with the fading initials E.M.P. (for Eric Morton Paget) on the lid indicating that it had once belonged to my grandfather. Opening it was to summon back my mother's spirit, and that of the aunt I never knew, for the heaps of tattered brown envelopes and superannuated files conjured the sisters' animated dialogue with every pen-stroke of their contents. Here were the letters that Celia and Mamaine had exchanged when apart – which, given Mamaine's peripatetic life with Arthur Koestler, in Wales, Paris, Palestine and America, were many and frequent, taking on the role of diaries in their eventful and sociable lives.

Here, too, were several cardboard folders that stopped me in my tracks: one of letters from Albert Camus, in French of course, that I had never properly deciphered: love letters to Mamaine, and deeply affectionate letters to Celia (and to his former rival Arthur) after Mamaine's death. At first, I found his handwriting difficult to read, but I soon picked up its idiom and his turn of phrase – it's strange how quickly that can happen. Only recently, tucked between other papers, did I find a tiny Wallace Heaton envelope ('By Appointment to H.M. The King') containing the undeveloped negatives of snaps of Camus that Mamaine had taken during their week exploring Provence together. Another folder contained letters and documents concerning George Orwell, including a copy of the infamous List of 'fellow travellers' that he compiled for my mother in 1949 while lying gravely ill in Cranham Nursing Home. At the bottom of the pile was a battered package addressed to Mamaine in wonky capital letters containing the passionate, ill-spelt and vivid letters – some recounting his intrepid travels throughout the Middle East – that her first lover, the flamboyant arch-bohemian Dick Wyndham, had sent her over the several years of their affair and beyond, from 1937 until his death in 1948. And envelopes of engaging correspondence with my mother from a host of later friends, Sacheverell Sitwell, Laurie Lee, Frances Partridge, Benjamin Britten and Peter Pears among them.

These relationships, and the letters which so vividly convey them, spanned the intense middle decades of the twentieth century – decades when the old order was shattered by war, and new ideas, beliefs and ways of living were emerging. Orwell, Koestler and Camus were at the epicentre of the great debates of the last century, between communism and anti-communism, freedom and totalitarianism. Although we once thought we had moved on and such titanic struggles would no longer occupy us to the same degree, we are again confronted today by their implications. The simple right to live one's own life, unchallenged, is not granted to millions the world over who live under repressive regimes. The freedom of the individual against the state is still fiercely contested, as is the right of a democracy such as Ukraine to exist in the face of totalitarian aggression. There is talk of a return to Cold War – and fear that it might be ignited into a global conflagration. These are no longer old arguments grown cold; their long shadow lies darkly among us, unavoidably current, and they are as worth fighting for now as they ever were.

Tenuously educated yet fiercely intelligent, and beautiful – famously so, and all the more striking for being identical – the Paget Twins, as they became widely known, took London by storm when they reluctantly 'came out' as debutantes in 1935. However, orphaned at the age of twelve and intrinsically unconventional, they were to find far greater happiness in the bohemian and challenging company of intellectuals than in the straitened grip of the Society life that their wealthy guardians had in mind for them. Once they gained their independence, they struck out on their own and made their lives among the preeminent writers and thinkers of the age, Orwell, Camus and Koestler among them.

As identical twins, they were completely and perfectly in tune with one another, and they shared passions and enthusiasms to a remarkable degree. Their talent and energy for friendship was exceptional: 'gregarious' is a word that might have been invented for them, but my mother preferred the term 'friendable'. Yet, despite a social life that I could barely keep up with when reading their appointment diaries, they both had rich inner lives, nourished by their curiously isolated childhood, their wide reading in several languages, and their passion for literature and music: both played the piano, practising, when they had time, for up to four hours a day. Whenever possible, they would seek out the silence (birdsong excepted) and relative solitude of the countryside as a counterpoint to their frenetic city days. As they acquired financial independence and carved out their own paths, the bohemian 'intellectual aristocracy' of the times became their milieu, the current in which they swam. Their diaries, and particularly the letters they exchanged whenever they were apart, vividly and amusingly convey the rollercoaster of their lives: the currents of thought and politics in which they were engaged, and passions requited and unrequited.

The twins came of age in an era menaced by the twin ideologies of communism and fascism. The Spanish Civil War had acted as the catalyst for Orwell's and Koestler's – among many others' – awakening to the evils of communism. Meanwhile, western Europe was, too slowly, gathering itself against the menace of fascism and slouching towards war. Post-1945, the world pivoted into an increasingly chilly Cold War. The twins' relationships with some of the protagonists, early cold warriors and passionate advocates for freedom, meant they were swept up in the tumultuous, manichean struggles of that era. These they chronicled, from the inside track, with wit and a degree of droll dispassion.

Luckily we have long moved beyond the 'great men' school of history, and have realised the value of teasing out of the shadows those other lives that constitute the warp and weft of any age – the formerly ignored and belittled 'footnotes in history'. For those who found themselves caught up in the crosswires also had lives deserving of attention, and rich and rewarding to explore. Mamaine and Celia may have played walk-on parts in the biographies of others, but here I hope to give them back their starring roles, and in doing so to fill in more pieces in the complex jigsaw puzzle of their era.

Modesty and discretion, that now almost discredited quality, lay behind Celia's decision never to write her own memoirs. And though she was generous in sharing her papers with researchers and biographers, she always kept the most personal mementoes back. But those papers and her memories, shared with me over so many years, cast such a personal, oblique and idiosyncratic light on the era in which they lived – and on the closely entwined lives of the twins – that they now seem to warrant their own moment in the sun, and she gave me her blessing to write about them.

•

In many people's lives there is an absent figure – dead, lost or mislaid – who exerts a powerful fascination – a 'significant other' in the dynamics of a family. Mamaine, the captivating aunt who died the year before my birth, was that figure in my childhood. I grew up under her spell, and as I've grown older I've felt ever more acutely the loss of not having known her. Her letters and diaries speak with such a distinctive voice – warm, quirky, amused and amusing – that I have always felt close to her, all the more so as they echo the timbre of my mother's voice. They speak of someone both courageous and frail, whose spirit, natural wit and passion enabled her to rise above considerable odds to make of her all-too-brief life something precious to all who knew her.

The defining relationship of Mamaine's life was with my mother Celia, her twin sister and only sibling. Loved by and loving others passionately, their deepest and most impregnable bond was nevertheless with one another: 'I have been to London for ten days, with the object of seeing Celia,' Mamaine wrote to the critic Edmund Wilson in 1948. 'My twinnie relationship is such that I can't go for long without talking to her – indeed I wonder what on earth I would do if K.[oestler] and I went to live in the States as we talk of doing.' After an extraordinarily close childhood, the twins were separated for long periods of their adult lives, at times living on different sides of the English Channel or the Atlantic Ocean. They wrote continually when apart, and crossed continents to be in one another's company.

They also shared a childhood heritage of acute anxiety, expressed in chronic asthma which dogged both their lives with periods of illness and suffering. There was a febrile quality about them – which, allied to their beauty and intensity, people found hard to resist. Celia was always thought to be the weaker of the two, and Mamaine was furiously protective of her; it was not until after the breakdown of her marriage to Arthur Koestler that Mamaine's health began seriously to deteriorate. It was as if the bright flame that had hitherto sustained her now flickered and finally failed. She died in 1954, at the age of thirty-seven, deeply mourned – but it is the brightness of her memory that I want to capture here, and the unassailable bond with her twin sister Celia, deeper than all the other loves, however intense, in a life so tragically cut short.

Writing in the early 2020s about an era several generations ago, before the second wave of feminism in the 1960s sent the tectonic plates sliding further, I find myself immersed in a world where men still called most of the shots, and women relied on their wits and intuition to negotiate as much autonomy as they desired. Some desired more autonomy than others; some achieved it. I'm making no value judgement from my vantage point well into the twenty-first century, with all the opportunities that I've benefited from.

In writing of Orwell, Camus and Koestler I am entering a crowded field, and an often contested one, but my guiding principle has been truth to the letters and diaries in my possession and to the stories that I grew up with. I hope the story I tell will resonate and be seen for what it attempts to be: a faithful family memoir, and an excursion to that foreign country where they certainly did things differently, and where many of the assumptions and principles to which we hold fast today were yet to be adopted.

THE DAZZLING
PAGET SISTERS

CHAPTER 1

GEMINI

Celia and Mamaine Paget were born in September 1916, and were orphaned by the age of twelve. Their mother Georgina, who gave birth to them at what was then the advanced age of forty-two, died one week later, agonisingly, of complications from the birth. Their father Eric Paget was already fifty, too old to be involved in the war that was raging on the Continent. Poleaxed by grief at the death of his beloved wife, he was plunged into despair. He had no experience as a father (an earlier daughter, Stella, had died soon after birth): what on earth was he to do with not one baby but two? How could he possibly cope? The twins were tiny and frail at birth and showed every sign of expiring in those first few weeks, so he had them quickly baptised at home as Mamaine and Celia Mary, fearing that he would lose them too. But to everyone's astonishment they pulled through.

Two months later he wrote a touching letter for Mollie (Celia) and Maimie, as he called them, to read one day, about his love for Georgina, their life together, the reasons for her death, and his hopes for the twins' happiness. It is couched in the Edwardian language of the day, restrained and underpinned by reverence:

> It is sad indeed for you, my dears, to be motherless – but she had the glory & happiness of dying in Victory […]. She longed for children – and had you two – She wanted love and I loved her with a love that was almost pain. Love and children fulfilled all the utmost of her earthly wishes. She had everything – then she died – Life after that with all its sorrows, stresses and anxiety would be an anti-climax. Most of all in this world she dreaded my death. Think what she had and what is left for me, my dears. Hadn't she Victory?

Eric, however, was left with the sorrows and anxiety; he had to find some help and somehow put his life back together, though he understandably lacked the energy or will. Luckily, he managed to find in Ellen Michelmore, the daughter of a Devon farmer, a stalwart, dignified nanny in the traditional mould: 'a true lady in thought and feeling', in Eric's words. She agreed to move in and take on the care of the twins, which she continued to do with long-suffering devotion until they were sent away to school at the age of eleven.

Sad and lonely as my grandfather Eric was after Georgina's death, he nevertheless grew to adore his comical little daughters. He was endlessly amused by them, inventing names and stories for their entertainment, and their antics brought laughter back into his life. He photographed them with his tripod camera as they grew from quaint

The twins with their father Eric Paget

mop-haired creatures into curious little girls, developing and printing the results himself. It is all but impossible to tell them apart in the photos – they were dressed identically as children and had the same heart-shaped faces and inquisitive eyes, the same mischievous and sometimes wistful expression. They were inseparable from the start and perfectly content in one another's company, devising endless games and stories, expeditions and adventures to fill their carefree childhood days.

While married, Eric and Georgina Paget had occupied the pretty, high-walled White Lodge in the centre of the village of Melton on the outskirts of Woodbridge, Suffolk, and were diffident but active participants in the life of the neighbourhood. Once widowed, however, Eric sold White Lodge and withdrew to the Old Schoolhouse on the road to Lower Ufford, where he had fewer visitors and took an ever-diminishing part in village activities. So there the twins grew up, odd but precocious, occupying a world they largely fashioned from their imagination. For company they had only their erudite, retiring father, their elderly nanny – whom they loved – the gardener, and an occasional visiting aunt to teach them to write and read, for they had no formal schooling until the age of seven. At that point the retired village schoolmaster, Mr Bentham, was appointed to walk up from the village and give them one hour of lessons a day. He made no concessions to their age, reading them a speech by Burke on the French Revolution as readily as an extract from Piers Plowman or *The Faerie Queen* or the poetry of Alfred Tennyson. The twins lapped it all up, and their deep enjoyment of the language and literature they encountered through Mr Bentham instilled in them a lifelong love of poetry. Naturally inquisitive, they learned more from him, my mother claimed, than any subsequent school ever managed to din into them.

Theirs was a simple and unsophisticated rural childhood, in sharp contrast to the smart and wealthy world they would enter upon their father's death. Both their father and mother were Pagets, but entirely unrelated, which was how they met: holidaying alone in Hyeres in 1910, Mr Paget was puzzled to receive a letter addressed to Miss Paget, and on delivering it to its rightful recipient Mr Eric Paget promptly fell in love with the beautiful, auburn-haired and unaccountably still unmarried Miss Georgina Paget. A swift courtship developed into a profound and lasting love. They were married fairly late by the standards of the day – Georgina was twenty-nine when they met – but theirs was a union of remarkable happiness.

Georgina's family were wealthy, landed gentry from Leicestershire, who counted among their ancestors one of the heroes of Waterloo, the Marquess of Anglesey, who was close to Wellington when he lost part of one leg to a cannonball, exclaiming, 'By God Sir, I've lost my leg!' 'By God Sir, so you have!' was Wellington's peremptory reply as he careered past on his horse – no point in wasting words in an emergency. Eric was descended from Lord Auckland, a Whig and First Lord of the Admiralty who served as Governor-General of India from 1836–42, at the disastrous start of the Great Game. Auckland's redoubtable sister the novelist Emily Eden (author of *The Semi-Detached House* and *The Semi-Attached Couple*) lost no time in joining him in India, staying on for six years and taking the opportunity to travel as far and wide as her stamina and supplies would take her. Her witty letters home charting her adventures on the road were published as *Up the Country*, and blazed a trail for independent, no-nonsense women who shot from the hip.[1] Eric's father had been vicar at Hoxne in the Waveney Valley, on the border of Suffolk and Norfolk. His wife gave birth to four sons but, unfortunately for her husband, she also conducted a long and not-entirely-discreet affair with the dashing local squire, Sir Edward Kerrison of nearby Oakley Park. Two of her sons were thought to have resulted from that union, Eric possibly among them, so our origins are shaded in uncertainty and we may indeed not be who we think we are – but is that so very unusual?

By the time of the twins' birth during the First World War, Eric and Georgina lived in comfortable but far from lavish style. Eric employed a cook called Mabel and a gardener as well as the twins' nanny – but the house was

plain, with oil lamps and coal fires, and their father owned no such new-fangled devices as a telephone or motorcar. Winter afternoons for the twins would be spent playing long games of patience, hammering out elaborate make-believe stories on Eric's typewriter, or listening, entranced, to his pianola. Their father's study was well stocked with books, and he would often read them chapters from Dickens, George Eliot or Arnold Bennett, whose novels they found enthralling. Above all, they enjoyed poring over the hand-painted illustrations for *Meyer's British Birds and Their Eggs,* which resulted in a lifelong passion for birds and birdsong. The woods around them were loud with the hoots and screeches of owls, wrens nested in the ivy-clad poplars and the canopied Scotch pines hummed with the soft cooing of wood pigeons. Perhaps because they had such a musical ear, or perhaps because they started young, both were able to recognise almost any bird from its song, and every country walk was enhanced and amplified by the soundtrack of birdsong, to the very end of my mother's life.

The long summers were largely spent outside, playing with their pets (a mongrel dog, a pet bullfinch and numerous guinea-pigs whose breeding activities were a source of endless fascination) and if at all possible prevailing upon their father ('Mr Sardine') to join them on a walk or a picnic, when he would carve bulrushes into candles for them, and entertain the twins with long stories of his own invention in which they featured as boys called Charlie (Celia) and Tuppity (Mamaine) – for  that is what they longed to be. Otherwise, they filled their days, indeed lost all count of time, stepping from stone to stone over the rock garden while holding elaborate conversations about the increasingly intractable meaning of life; or scampering down to the banks of the River Deben, which could be seen down the fields from the end of their garden; or thrashing through the bird-filled woods and hedgerows.

The twins saw a few children from the village, but without school they had no schoolfriends, and no regular social life – certainly nothing orchestrated by Eric on their behalf. Eric was unworldly and quite out of touch with the latest fads and trends, as was their nanny, so Mollie and Maimie were dressed in odd, unfashionable clothes. Increasingly, they loathed dolls and dresses, and, on being

lent a dolls' pram, they immediately overturned it, hurling its inmates out onto the lawn, and stuffed it with books to trundle about with instead. When they were five they were taken to a blind barber who, under the mistaken

With boys' haircuts
after a trip to the barber

9

impression that they were twin boys, gave them both short-back-and-sides haircuts, much to their delight.

Their greatest passion was music, from an early age – they listened endlessly to their father's pianola rolls, which included the Waldstein Sonata and the Spinning Song from *The Flying Dutchman,* and encouraged him to sing or whistle his large repertoire of Gilbert and Sullivan songs. Apart from this, they attended dancing lessons at nearby Boulge Hall (once home of Edward Fitzgerald, translator of the Omar Khayyam) where they heard their first snatches of piano music, and soaked up the hymns and psalms sung in the local church. But they had never been taken to a concert or show, so a surprise trip when they were ten to the 1926 Dolmetsch Early Music Festival at Haslemere with their kind relation Alice Edwardes rated as the high point of their childhood. The early music, played on contemporary instruments or reproductions of them, was a revelation to the twins, as was the sophisticated conversation of the coterie of Early Music buffs who congregated there – Gerald Hayes and the intrepid traveller and Buddhist Marco Pallis, one of the earliest westerners to report back from Tibet, among them. And they were transfixed by the Dolmetsch family themselves, all of whom performed together on different instruments in traditional costume: so much so that the twins wrote a 'novel' about them, which has not survived – more's the pity. Altogether, the excitement of musical discovery and the company of such cultured people was a revelation to two intensely musical children, starved of any real classical repertoire and live performance.

Into their essentially happy if uneventful childhood –
which left them with an abiding love of the landscape of
rural Suffolk – edged a cloud of gathering dread. When
the twins were seven, their father made a rare expedition
to London and returned with an extra hint of gravity: he
had been to see a specialist and the news was not good.
He told the twins nothing of course, but they gleaned
from his altered mood, his sombre stance when caught
off-guard, that something was amiss, and they were
assailed with a deep sense of foreboding. Eric had been
told he was suffering from an incurable disease of the central nervous system (most likely Parkinson's) and that his
life expectancy was not long. However much he tried to
conceal it, his melancholia drew him further into himself
as he became physically frailer and his nerves took on a
rawer edge. The twins' worst suspicions were confirmed
when they overheard their father say to a man in the village, 'When I die you must take over the bowls club.' It

With Ellen Michelmore and Mr King, the gardener

was shortly after this that both Mollie and Maimie, whose lungs had never been strong, developed chronic asthma, which can be psychosomatic in origin, and from that moment neither was ever free from its malignant grasp, which waxed and waned in intensity over the course of their often turbulent lives.

They could only look on, powerless, as their father's health and spirits grew fainter, and by the time they were nine it was evident that he had not long to live. He had written annual letters for the twins to read when they were grown-up enough to understand them, reiterating the depth of his love for them and his hopes for their future: 'My darlings do try to live unselfish lives and let a sense of humour help you in all your troubles,' he exhorted when they were only three and a half. Now, in 1925, he admits in his last letter to them:

I have a good lot of pain now, but it seems to make me love you all the more. You are TARTARS just now; you are cracked about birds as you were last year. This year you are several degrees worse. The worst of it is you crawl about in the ivy & give Nanny & me fits. . . . BLESSINGS TO YOU MY DARLINGS What larks we have had together YOUR LOVING MISTER SARDINE.

Shortly after writing this he admitted himself to Chiswick nursing home, from which he was never to emerge alive, and the twins were sent away, in great distress, to the first of a disastrous series of boarding schools. It is not hard to imagine their anguish – torn away from their ailing father and fond, dependable nanny, the only home they had ever known, their secluded Suffolk life, and thrown into a maelstrom of strange and none-too-friendly girls in a hideous institution in Epping Forest. Had they not had one another for consolation, my mother told me, they would surely have had some sort of breakdown.

They were consumed with fear for their father's fate and for their own future, and spent most of the time playing truant and roaming the surrounding fields and woods. As my mother recalled, 'We learned nothing at all there, because we were in no mood for concentration. Every morning we made our way to the fields beyond the grounds and wandered about in them until sunset or until we felt our absence might be detected. Owing to the haphazard nature of the school timetable it almost always remained unnoticed . . .' It was not a policy calculated to endear them to either girls or teachers – and there were several

With their dog Scrap

nasty incidents in the dorm involving various kinds of rit-
ual humiliation and bullying – but the twins were beyond
caring. They learned little, and they contributed even less,
but they needed all their mutual strength just to bear the
freight of their own grief and foreboding.

The worst happened, in due course: after a year, Alice
Edwardes (the cousin who had introduced them to the
Dolmetsch Festival) took them out of school to tell them
that their father had died. Added to their intense sadness
was a profound sense of abandonment, and a feeling that
the entire structure of their lives had been summarily with-
drawn, leaving them 'howling in space', as Henry James
put it in a different context. As if that were not devastating enough, they were to become the legal wards of
near-strangers: their wealthy uncle Jack Paget (their mother's only brother) and his French wife Germaine, who had
two daughters – Wynnie, three years older than they, and

Anne, three years younger – and lived in a vast house called Ibstock Place in fashionable Roehampton. During their father's illness they had spent some time over the holidays with these glamorous relatives, but nevertheless it was a daunting prospect for two now-desolate country cousins, as they felt themselves to be. There was nowhere else for them to go, however, and their aunt and cousins embraced them with genuine warmth and generosity, so they had no option but to make the best of it.

CHAPTER 2

THE TWO OF US

Now Celia and Mamaine abruptly entered another world, making a discordant break with the past. It was like stepping down the proverbial rabbit hole, and finding all aslant, contingent, unfamiliar. The simple frugality of their childhood gave way to ostentatious plenty; the predictable rhythm of Suffolk days was replaced by jarring novelty at every turn.

Ibstock Place is a large and attractive Queen Anne–style mansion on the edge of Richmond Park, now home to a successful independent school. Uncle Jack had purchased the building in 1925 (it was formerly inhabited by the Duchess of Sutherland) and furnished it lavishly with a set of Louis XVI Aubusson tapestries and a Bluthner grand piano – a surprising purchase since he and his family were all tone-deaf. Fascinated as he was by 'modern gadgets', he installed a telephone exchange, reputedly the first in Britain, and sunk one of the first private swimming pools in the extensive terraced gardens. The twins found themselves enveloped in luxury, attended to by phalanxes of servants – there were eighteen staff, including a butler whose head was higher on one side than the other, to look

Ibstock Place in the 1930s

after a family which, even after the twins arrived, numbered just six. It was all baffling to Celia and Mamaine, who took several weeks to work out who was who, and what their various duties were.

The twins' aunt Germaine, known until her dying day as Ging-Ging, was irresistible – descended from an ancient French family, the de Beaunés, she was spirited and fascinating, a friend in her youth of Coco Chanel and once an habituée of the smartest set in Paris. Brought up in the kind of aristocratic Belle Époque society described by Proust, she was nevertheless entirely devoid of snobbery or vanity, and as a young woman she charmed all who met her and had suitors in droves. She had an irreverent sense of humour and could be very amusing, her strongly French-accented conversation peppered with malapropisms, such as saying that

17

someone was 'in death's store' rather than 'at death's door'.

All the more extraordinary, then, that she had married the chilly if eligible Englishman Jack Paget at the age of nineteen, leaving behind her glamorous youth in Paris. She evidently did not find life with him easy; he was the fly in the ointment at Ibstock Place. By the time the twins entered his household, Jacko (as they privately called Uncle Jack) was the very epitome of the British army major (retired): tall, straight and stiff, with monocle and moustache, and a baleful eye. His draconian diktats and wild swings of mood often terrorised the household, and Ging-Ging and the four girls were united in alarm and apprehension. Even Ging-Ging, who made light of most things, found it hard to keep her end up and became

increasingly nervous as the wearying years of marital proximity took their toll.

The more the twins discovered about him, the stranger Uncle Jack revealed himself to be: a deeply eccentric figure, riven with contradictions. His ancestors had owned mines in Derbyshire, and he was fabulously wealthy, but like many people who inherit rather than achieve their wealth in person he could be extremely stingy. As children we revelled in Celia's stories of his footling economies: how he always travelled First Class while consigning his family to steerage; how he insisted on low-wattage lightbulbs and other trivia, leading the twins to nickname their opulent new home Poverty Hall. However, he could be as generous with strangers as he was parsimonious at home, writing extravagant and often anonymous cheques to unsuspecting charities, and paying for miners who were suffering from lung diseases to holiday luxuriously in the Alps or recuperate in sanatoria. He took a shine to Eglantyne Jebb, founder of Save the Children ('Just my type of gal,' I can imagine him saying), and sent her a cheque for ten thousand pounds (equivalent now to £750,000), pinned to an advertisement roughly torn from a daily paper. This electrified the charity, putting it on a firm footing for many decades to come.

Jacko was also a vegetarian, theosophist, and a believer in astrology, fortune-telling and reincarnation, which led him to come up with a hypothesis that his youngest daughter, Anne, had been William Pitt the Younger in a former life. (A portrait of William Pitt hung in the dining room, and he had measured the dimensions of Pitt's skull, compared it with that of his youngest daughter, and drawn this surprising conclusion.) When Anne was summoned downstairs, aged twelve, to prove this was the case by regaling a lunch party with accounts of speeches she had supposedly given in the House, but was unable to perform, he sheepishly conceded that he might have been mistaken. He was, by any definition of the word,

A 1930s period piece: Ging-Ging with Wynnie and Anne (above and below left) and the twins, photographed by Yevonde for *Tatler*, February 1933

a genuine eccentric, both imperious and insensitive in laying down the law on every subject. Wynnie and Anne had fortunately inherited their mother's warmth, kindness and humour, and did all they could to make life in the schoolroom more congenial for the bewildered twins, but it was a painful period of adjustment, and Jacko's beady and menacing presence did nothing to console them for their precipitate uprooting from Suffolk and relocation to an unfamiliar world.

Uncle Jack was a Conservative of the deepest dye and would have thought the twins Traitors to their Class had he even suspected the depth of their nascent liberal convictions. Readable books, their lifeline, were in vanishingly short supply at Ibstock Place, and while the twins were shown every kindness by Ging-Ging and their cousins, they felt completely out of their element. The rolling, deer-studded expanses of Richmond Park lay at their doorstep, yet they could not help pining for the rough patchwork of fields and hedgerows, the banks of the River Deben that had run past their childhood home, and the marsh rushes swaying in the wind. I realise that this might make the twins sound sullen and ungrateful, but the simple fact was that they were distraught at the abrupt and irretrievable change to their circumstances.

Celia and Mamaine changed schools but were no less unhappy at the new one, near Malden in Essex, and were amazed and alarmed at the cattiness that girls could show to one another. Angelica Garnett, daughter of Duncan Grant and Vanessa Bell, was an intriguing fellow pupil, exquisite, quiet and friendly, unlike the 'large, fat stupid girl called Porky who was bribed to swing us around by our hair and put us down on hot radiators, which on account of our small size she was easily able to do'. They pleaded to be taken away, and luckily their increasingly precarious health persuaded a doctor to recommend that they should be sent to Switzerland, where the air was dry and their asthmatic lungs could recover. So they were dispatched, aged fifteen, to a *pensionnat de jeunes filles,* or finishing school, above Lausanne in the Swiss Alps. After their two English boarding schools, this one seemed like Paradise – mainly because it was full of friendly and high-spirited Europeans and Americans instead of their dour or bitchy classmates back home.

Rather than sleeping in a noisy, cramped dormitory, they shared a pretty bedroom overlooking the Lake of Geneva, where the lights of Evian sparkled on the opposite shore. They quickly picked up conversational French and a smattering of German and Italian from the other girls, and opened up like flowers in their cosmopolitan company. Gradually, their health improved in the crisp dry air of the mountains, and they emerged from the sad and anxious state of mind that their father's death had plunged them into. Altogether, the three years they spent in Lausanne were happy ones, during which they found their feet and their voices. Ever after, the Alpine landscape – to which they returned whenever they could – would summon up health and high spirits. They even managed to procure some lessons in music and the history of ideas among the otherwise dim options on the curriculum, but this finishing-school tuition was never going to be good enough to equip them for the university education they longed to have.

They left Lausanne in the summer of 1934, now determined to learn better Italian and German to supplement their almost fluent French. German – the language of Rilke and Hölderlin, of Schubert and Schumann, Strauss and Mahler; Italian, for the sheer, fluid delight of it, the lilting beauty of its tones and phrases. Their years in Switzerland had made them thoroughly European in outlook, like so many of their generation, and they longed to travel more widely, despite the gathering menace of fascism in Italy, Spain and Germany. Through friends, they soon found themselves a *pensione* in Florence run by a German family, most of whose guests were elderly German Jewish refugees, in whose company they felt completely at home. That spring of 1935, which they spent surrounded by a group of Italian friends and two delightful young German admirers who squired them around, often in horse-drawn *carrozze*, was the happiest they could remember. They explored the city from Fiesole to Porta Romana, the scent of mimosa always in the air, the lazy days spent familiarising themselves with the beauty of the churches and palazzi punctuated by concerts at the Teatro Communale and in the Sala Bianca at the Palazzo Pitti. The only cloud on the horizon was the prospect of their return to England, since their fervent wish to go to university had been overruled in favour of the then fashionable custom of 'coming out'. Uncle Jacko and Ging-Ging thought the mere notion of university for girls preposterous. They were not alone: for many of their generation and social class, marriage to someone of the right breeding was the only acceptable goal, to be achieved as swiftly and efficiently as possible through the byzantine workings of the Season.

My mother sometimes quoted – with irony – Queen Victoria, who is reputed to have said, 'What's all this damned nonsense about education? The Pagets have got on very well without it.' In fact, like many women of their generation, she and Mamaine came to feel that its formal lack was a permanent disadvantage, though thanks to their natural intelligence and curiosity, the milieu they moved into and the books they read, they were able to hold their own in almost any company, however elevated.

Still, their lives and careers could have been so different had they been granted that bedrock of schooling they desired, and had they been allowed to go to university, a concept as alien to their guardians as flying to the moon. The twins were natural-born bluestockings, as it happened – though they would hardly have recognised the word, and would have laughed it off had they done so. Celia was, in consequence, determined that I should have the best education available, at whatever cost, in order to escape the constraints that she felt had hobbled her own career – though, by the standards of the time, her various roles in journal publishing and intelligence were hardly insignificant. But, in 1935, as Uncle Jack and Ging-Ging summoned them back to England, they had no alternative but to buckle down with as good a grace as they could muster, and steel themselves for what lay in store.

CHAPTER 3

SOCIETY AND
ITS DISCONTENTS

Much has been written about the arcane world of the debutante, shepherded from ball to ball, fork lunch to tea party
to cocktail party to dinner party, by mothers or chaperones
who filled their wards' days and diaries with steely determination. After the twins' presentation at Court in late
March 1935 – wearing 'identical gowns of rich ivory moiré
taffeta with draped off-the-shoulder décolletage and posies
of blush pink roses on one shoulder' as several newspapers
gushed – there were nightly dances five days a week at the
height of the Season.

Often several dances took place on a single night,
requiring deft planning and considerable stamina to get
from one to another and remember which was which, let
alone who at each new extravaganza was who. For, despite
their undoubted splendour, these parties merged into a
haze of flower-bedecked ballrooms, chandeliers, corsages,
champagne, and crowds of fresh-faced girls and chipper
young men whirling the evenings away.

Uncle Jack and Ging-Ging did their own share of
entertaining, with frequent garden, bathing and tennis
parties, or sometimes all three merged into one, as reported

THE MISSES CELIA AND MAIMAINE PAGET, the attractive twin daughters of the late Mr. and Mrs. Eric M. Paget, who were presented at the Second Court on Friday of last week. They are relatives of the Marquess of Anglesey

Presentation at Court – for the twins, a regrettable rite of passage breathlessly in July 1935 under the heading 'The Perfect Garden Party':

> One of the loveliest gardens in London, that of Ibstock Place, Mrs J.B. Paget's beautiful Roehampton Home, was the perfect setting for a large garden party recently.
>
> In a gown of pale blue, Mrs Paget received the guests, who numbered close on a thousand. Bathing in the pool, watching a water polo match and tennis were the principal entertainments. The Paget Twins Celia and Mamaine, in blue and white bathing suits, were two of the most energetic swimmers.[2]

The twins did love dancing, swimming and tennis, and managed to find a few congenial companions among the throng, but in their eyes the whole Season was a regrettable rite of passage, to be endured through gritted teeth. The endless social whirl left no time to do any of the things they frankly preferred: riding and reading and playing the piano. Photos of them from this period show them posed and made up: ravishing, yes, but an expression of sullen resignation in their eyes has replaced their natural animation. In the camera's lens, they look cool to the point of unapproachability.

Neither twin had any intention of falling in love with any of their dancing partners, which rather undermined the whole enterprise. 'Oh, the boredom,' my mother would groan at the memory, 'of getting dressed up every night for yet another pointless ball, when we were never going to marry any of the men we met there. Then spending most

Mamaine and Celia

of the morning in bed sleeping it off before starting all over again for the next one . . . And as "Debutantes of the Year" we had to go through the whole thing not once, but twice,' she added in exasperation. She might have added that they were darlings of the newspapers, too, which fawned and photographed them at every available opportunity.

It was as my mother said – despite their evident popularity, and the splash they made as identical twins, they managed to avoid being snapped up during the first of their Seasons, so, ever optimistic, Ging-Ging forced them to repeat the whole farrago the following year. They had no means of refusing, given their indebtedness to their uncle and aunt, but they did manage to make a few friends on the circuit who felt as rebellious as they did. Jessica ('Decca') Mitford, sixth of the seven Mitford siblings, was among them; in her memoir *Hons and Rebels* she remembered the sea of 'smooth, fair guileless faces, radiating the health bestowed by innumerable fresh-air-filled upbringings in innumerable country houses' of those parties. It would be easier, she thought, to distinguish the faces of Australian sheep . . .[3]

Like the twins, she was impervious to the charms of her sheep-faced suitors, particularly as she was already smitten with the idea of her cousin Esmond Romilly, Churchill's nephew and, at the age of eighteen, a dyed-in-the-wool rebel, pacifist and communist. His attraction was only enhanced by his having been sentenced to six weeks in a remand home for delinquent boys after showing up drunk at his parents' house, and she couldn't wait to meet him, even contemplating becoming a prison visitor to achieve this end more quickly. She converted to communism in sympathy, and, when she finally met Esmond, just back from a stint fighting in Spain with the Republicans, it was a foregone conclusion that they would become inseparable. She lost no time in imploring him to take her back to Spain with him. They laid careful plans to run away together, and it was the twins she gave as her alibi.

On learning that Celia and Mamaine were off to the Austrian Alps for a while – so there was no danger that her mother, Lady Redesdale or 'Muv', would run across them in London – she and Esmond came up with a plan to pretend that Decca had been invited to stay with the twins in Dieppe, where Ging-Ging was supposed to have taken a house. Dieppe was handily in the direction of Spain, so Decca could conserve her carefully husbanded Running Away Fund by claiming the fare as far as Dieppe from Muv. Decca and Esmond jointly forged a letter from the twins, painting an irresistible picture of a house by the sea, boys from Oxford coming over in a rented motor

Celia

Mamaine

car to tour around (this a master stroke of Esmond's, to allow for bulletins from other French towns as they journeyed south), all to be presided over by the twins' impeccably respectable French aunt. Celia always claimed that Decca had a touch of the delinquent about her – she was ruthless and would stop at nothing to get her way – and Esmond even more so; they were the perfect match. So the young lovers made it over to France, and south to Bayonne, posting letters en route, 'Having a lovely time with the twins . . .', 'We are now touring France in a car brought by one of the boys from Oxford' and suchlike, to allay suspicions back home.

Contrary to these sunny missives, life in Bilbao, when they arrived there in February 1937, was unremittingly grim. The town was starving, and Decca was consumed with anxiety about what must be happening at home in Rutland Gate, where she imagined Mitford family life flowing smoothly on – or had they rumbled her? As it turned out, they had. The twins were skiing in Austria and entirely oblivious of the ruse, as was Ging-Ging, who remained firmly at home in Ibstock Place and was astonished to receive a call from a flustered Muv, who had put a call through to Dieppe only to find it a false trail. There followed a 'mystifying conversation full of cross-purposes' between Ging-Ging and Lady Redesdale, culminating in the revelation that Decca had apparently vanished without trace.

Scotland Yard and the Foreign Office were called in, and, when the lovers' whereabouts and – even worse – plans for marriage were finally ascertained, Farve (Baron Redesdale) detonated like a bomb. The Proconsul in Bilbao revealed to the runaways that he had received a coded telegram from the Foreign Secretary, Anthony Eden: 'FIND JESSICA MITFORD AND PERSUADE HER TO RETURN,' to which the lovers coolly dictated the Proconsul's coded reply: 'HAVE FOUND JESSICA MITFORD, IMPOSSIBLE TO PERSUADE HER TO RETURN.' Decca's older sister Nancy and her husband, Peter Rodd, were then dispatched by boat to St Jean de Luz to retrieve Decca from Esmond and certain infamy. In this they failed, returning to England empty-handed, while the lovers stayed on in Bayonne, Esmond eking out a living by interpreting dispatches from the Basque front. Eventually, they managed to get permission to be married by the British Consul. Their disapproving mothers reluctantly came out to Bayonne for the wedding, sitting hatchet-faced throughout the ceremony, but cheered up in time for a jolly wedding lunch.

The whole episode sounds a droll and typically delinquent jape on Decca's part, but it was no laughing matter at the time: it was as if there had been a death in the family during the frantic days before Decca's whereabouts were discovered. My mother recalled visiting the vast and gloomy Rutland Gate at this time for, on returning home, the twins could not but feel implicated in Decca's ruse. Calling on a distraught Lady Redesdale to offer their commiserations, they found the house buzzing like a hive, and Decca's younger sister Debo, then a ravishingly pretty seventeen-year-old, dispassionately surveying the commotion from the depths of an armchair. It was like a funeral, Nancy recalled later, with Muv wringing her hands and Nanny worrying about the state of Decca's underwear, and flowers and visitors arriving every few minutes. And, indeed, at a time when international telephone lines were unreliable and telegrams (or the lack of them) the sole means of swift communication, it was all too easy for someone to disappear off the map, causing heartbreak to those at home left wondering about their fate.

Two Seasons down, and still stubbornly un-engaged, it was with infinite relief that the twins swapped the nightly balls and their roster of dapper but dreary dancing partners for the altogether more cultured, if raffish, company of Mamaine's new admirer Guy Richard Wyndham, known to all as Dick. Dick played for the twins the role that Esmond Romilly had played for Decca, opening doors into a fresh new world from which they never returned. History does not relate how he met Mamaine, but their encounter sparked the instant, magnetic attraction of opposites: Dick, twenty years older and very much a man of the world, Mamaine as yet unfledged, but eager for all that life could offer. Dick, twice divorced, was the magnetic centre of a circle that included the writers Cyril Connolly, Peter Quennell and Sacheverell Sitwell, composers William Walton and Constant Lambert and the painter Matthew Smith. When in London, the Café Royal, the Gargoyle Club or the Savoy Grill were their nightly haunts; at weekends, large gatherings would go down to Tickerage Mill, Dick's beautiful, secluded retreat in the midst of the Sussex Downs near Uckfield, for legendary house parties, bathing parties, croquet parties, fancy-dress parties, even eel-fishing parties. Nothing was off-limits, and Dick's wealth, and his generosity with his exceptionally well-stocked wine cellar, fuelled it all.

Dick Wyndham was effortlessly, unconsciously bohemian. Born in 1896, he was the wealthy son of Guy Percy Wyndham, soldier, Conservative Member of Parliament and prominent member of the group of intellectuals, politicians and aesthetes known as the Souls. Dick was brought up at Clouds, the capacious family house at East Knoyle in Wiltshire that had been commissioned in 1876 by his grandparents Percy and Madeline Wyndham from the Arts and Crafts architect Philip Webb. Philip Webb had been a radical and visionary choice; the Wyndhams differed from many of their aristocratic peers in the keen interest they took in the contemporary arts and in matters of taste. They wanted a 'house of the age' to become 'a palace of week-ending for our politicians' and their friends, and they furnished the newly risen many-bedroomed house with the latest in art and design. Arthur Balfour, Edward Burne-Jones, Herbert Asquith and Venetia Stanley were frequent guests, and life at Clouds revolved around the intense discussions, the flirtations and love affairs, the passions and obsessions of that somewhat overheated group. Together with their Tennant, Wemyss and Charteris cousins, the Wyndhams led a life of immense privilege, unbounded by convention. For them, ideas were more important than rules, and they boldly experimented with alternative ways to experience life to the full, happily sacrificing respectability to intensity of feeling.

After schooling at Wellington College and a stint at Sandhurst, Dick had served in the First World War with distinction, winning the Military Cross. He returned, however, half-crazy from his wartime experience, and his life thereafter would never fit into the conventional landowner

Dick Wyndham in Budapest

brief. Always devil-may-care and oblivious to his own physical safety, he was passionate about fast cars, racehorses and
light aircraft, relishing speed over caution every time. In
1914, Dick had inherited the estate at Clouds, and after
the war he moved in and started to enjoy his inheritance,
before tiring of its grandeur and swapping Clouds for the
modest but more beguiling Tickerage Mill.

A first marriage to Iris Bennett was over in a trice but
produced a daughter called Joan – later to titillate society
with her racy diaries of wartime London, published as *Love
Lessons* and *Love Is Blue* – and he was as unable to resist
beautiful women as he was allergic to commitment. As
his younger half-brother, the writer and publisher Francis
Wyndham, put it,

> His money was spent on racing cars, aeroplanes, a
> famous wine cellar, a collection of 'modern' pictures
> and series of difficult, exquisite girls. He enjoyed
> among his contemporaries a comfortable reputa-
> tion for privileged Bohemianism, scandalising some
> by his 'arty' inclinations, but avoiding the kind of
> unpopularity that might threaten his status as a
> proud member of Whites Club.[4]

Encouraged by his father, Guy, Dick decided he wanted
to become an artist, and studied under Harold Speed and
Wyndham Lewis, whom he met in Venice in 1922 and
with whom he developed a close but volatile friendship,
acting as both pupil and patron. Lewis taught him to
sketch the palaces in Venice, where Dick was holidaying
with Nancy Cunard, William Walton and the Sitwells, and

which, he reported back to Iris, 'is an incredibly beautiful place – too good for humanity it ought to be the capital of heaven'.[5] Dick had talent and determination, and exhibited regularly at London's more prominent galleries. He had bold taste and a good eye, and collected voraciously, often with the help of his friend Freddy Mayor of the Mayor Gallery, buying works by the likes of Giorgio de Chirico and Gino Severini well before the British public caught up with them. As well as his racehorses, he was reported by 'Londoners Diary' to keep a pet baby alligator called Queen Maud: 'She lives in a glass house, but enjoys nothing more than being taken out riding on her master's shoulder.' I never heard Celia mention Queen Maud, but such a story was typical of the mythic aura that accrued around Dick, combining heady rumours of excess and eccentricity.

It is almost too clichéd to describe him as tall, rugged and lantern-jawed, yet to judge from the photographs, that is what he was. He also possessed an irresistible, raffish charm.

Tickerage Mill

Described by Ian Fleming as 'a fine, careless figure, larger and more varied than the life around him', he was at the epicentre of the so-called 'Bright Young People', and divided his time between London and Tickerage, where he recreated on a smaller scale the lifestyle he had abandoned at Clouds. There were half

Rolling gardens at Tickerage

a dozen bedrooms, and he built himself a studio at the end of the house. He kept a housekeeper and a personal servant called Squib, and, although he claimed that when he was there alone he lived entirely on boiled cod, he was a natural *bon viveur* and a generous host, and enjoyed nothing more than entertaining friends with lavish weekend parties, where they played croquet in their pyjamas, dined deliciously and talked late into the night over an endless relay of fine clarets. Dick himself consumed an astonishing amount of alcohol without ever getting drunk. Friendships and love affairs wound and unwound at Tickerage, all presided over with benign insouciance by Dick, who was likened by Cyril Connolly, a frequent visitor, to 'an uncouth schoolboy [...] a Sargent drawing of the 1914 subaltern come to life'.[6]

Dick recalled his own first sight of Tickerage in 1926:

In a wooded valley lay a mill pool – silver among silver reeds, and bulrushes just bursting in white cotton cascade. Mallard and wild duck rose vertically from the marsh; a heron flopped from the great oak to perch ridiculously on top of the purple wood. The mill house was empty, and almost lost among unpruned apple trees, and gooseberry bushes run wild; a simple tile-hung cottage that for four hundred years had refused to fall down.[7]

When I visited, many decades later, Tickerage had lost none of its charm. Tucked away in the folds of the hills, on the course of a millstream, no one not invited to visit would have known it was there. To reach it, you plunged down a steep and narrow lane from the village of Blackboys, through woods which in May were full of bluebells and birdsong. The bridge over the millpond led to a long, low cottage which Dick often let or lent to friends for amorous escapes from the city, giving it its name The Love Nest. The Mill itself was to the right, a pretty red-brick house

The jetty

in front of which lawns planted with apple trees sloped down to the water. This lawn doubled as a croquet pitch, and John Piper told Celia how amused he was on his first visit to find a game of croquet being valiantly played uphill. The branches of these apple trees were full of tree-pipits in summer, which flung themselves into the air and drifted down again, uttering their seductive song.

By 1936, Dick had enjoyed a brief second skirmish with marriage, to the Norwegian model Greta Wulfsburg. This liaison lasted no longer than the first, but he and Greta remained on easy and affectionate terms: Dick was simply not cut out for marriage and fatherhood, and there were no hard feelings on either side.

I have dwelt in detail on Dick's background and personality because meeting him was the pivot in the twins' lives. Through him they encountered the literary, musical and artistic world which appeared to be their natural habitat, and they never looked back. A new circle of friends, a different set of values, the wide-open possibility of freedom – to be themselves, to fly in the face of stifling convention, to establish their independence at last.

One of this new circle was Dick's closest friend Sacheverell (Sachie) Sitwell, younger brother of Osbert and Edith, and by 1936 already an avowed aesthete, poet, critic, passionate advocate of the Rococo and Baroque, and author of books on Liszt and Scarlatti. He was wholly ingenuous; on one occasion Dick and Celia managed to drag him into a pub and he was quite flummoxed, having never set foot in such a place before. 'What shall I order?' he asked them, 'Quarter of a pint?' Married to the beautiful and chic Canadian heiress Georgia Doble, with whom he had fathered two young sons named Reresby and Francis, he and Georgia enjoyed an open marriage, both taking lovers along the way. Sachie now developed a powerful crush on Celia, expressed in teasing and whimsical letters that pursued her round Europe on her travels: 'I loved getting your letter, and was so amused by your handwriting. You've no idea how much I enjoyed seeing you last week, as I love making a new friend! [...] I do feel so grateful to Dick!' He told her he would get her handwriting analysed so that he could understand her better on her return and sent her books. While she was staying in Germany, he wrote to advise, 'Don't forget to go and see the wonderful rococo churches at Ettal and Wils, especially, and Rottenbach [...] don't stay away too long. I'm already longing to see you again, love Sachie.' She was still abroad when he acknowledged the twins' closeness in looks, writing, 'Give my best love to Mamaine [...] And do be careful not to get even the slightest shade more plump than you were in Dec: because that will make you quite unrecognisable from Mamaine, and you must keep your-selves to yourselves somehow or other.'

Their friendship grew, bolstered by the sharing of books and recordings. Late in 1938 he wrote to her in Germany:

Darling Celia [...] I am so glad you are enjoying yourself, and are feeling happy. I am not frightfully happy myself, as I have toothache, and as I am never frightfully happy anyway, or so it would seem. We go tomorrow to Switzerland [...] I think a lot about your new top hat, which I love so – also, probably more than I ought to, about you, for I am so very, very fond of you, and even nearly adore you, and as for 'trying to get at you', I should be very ashamed of myself if I did not. Still, there are ways and means of doing so; and I am sure I understand your moods enough to make you know how devoted I am to you. How much I wish I was talking to you now.

My New Year resolution for 1939 is to try not to be so fond of Celia, but am doubtful about its success, and certainly any more top hats will cause me to break the vow. [...] Best love from Sachie.

The friendship never progressed into romance but it meant a great deal to Celia, too, who relished Sachie's effortless erudition, his passions for architecture and classical music, his keen sense of humour, and his curious aquiline looks. The breadth of Sachie's enthusiasms, allied to his cosmopolitan familiarity with Europe and all it had to offer, was intoxicating. Their friendship continued until the day Sachie died, with Georgia's wary oversight; they would correspond regularly, visit one another when they could, and Sachie would send Celia every one of the countless books he wrote, and later the slim self-published poetry collections he compiled year-by-year.

As children, my brother and I would be taken to visit Sachie and Georgia at Weston Hall, their imposing manor house in Northamptonshire, where the alarming Georgia presided over richly ornamented but faded interiors that seemed to hark back to distant centuries, and we felt enveloped in a soft cloak of the past. Sachie's *coup de theatre* was showing us the 'haunted harp' which had belonged to the composer John Field and had been found by the butler one day playing by itself in an otherwise empty room.

More enjoyably, in 1975, Celia and I met up with him on a trip to Venice and were treated to drinks and ices at Florian's, before Sachie, then a spry seventy-six-year-old, took off like the White Rabbit in search of his favourite painting by Cima de Conegliano, the 'Baptism of Christ' in the church of San Giovanni in Bragora, with the two of us almost sprinting to keep up. His passion was undimmed, his charm still high-voltage, his air of faint melancholy concealing a wry sense of humour, and he made those days in Venice sparkle, as well as introducing me to a painter I had hitherto no idea existed.

Mamaine, meanwhile, was drawn ever more deeply into Dick Wyndham's sphere. Here was another 'difficult, exquisite girl', but one whom he would swiftly grow to adore. This came as something of a surprise to Dick, for he was well known as a roué, and a man who treated women with scant respect. He was used to playing the field and embarked on numerous transitory affairs which never troubled his conscience.

With Mamaine, however, it was different, as his letters attest. He grew to love her with a consuming passion, and although this love may not have entirely cured him of his habitual promiscuity, he came to see her as his one source of true happiness. Francis Wyndham claimed that Mamaine was the only woman Dick ever really loved. They enjoyed a perfect rapport in many ways and were never happier than when staying quietly at Tickerage together, he painting, she reading or birdwatching, interspersed with walks in the nearby woods. Then he would be lured by London's siren song and resume his furious social life, upon which tensions and rows would inevitably flare between them. The fact that he was a generation older than Mamaine and so much more worldly, coupled with his sophistication and insouciance, threatened to overwhelm her, and there were countless rifts and reunions, even before the war interrupted their lives and sent Dick around the country on army duties.

Nevertheless, the twins embraced Dick's London circle with relief after the banalities of the debutante whirl, and thrived in this more raffish company. Their new friends, through Dick, included the waspish Cyril Connolly, poised on the brink of his defining role as editor of the magazine *Horizon,* launched with the backing of the wealthy aesthete (and heir of a margarine fortune) Peter Watson;

Dick (left) in 1936 with Jean Bakewell, her husband Cyril
Connolly, Peter Quennell and his wife Marcelle

the poet, essayist and *flâneur* Peter Quennell, biographer of Baudelaire and Byron; the writer Henry Yorke (author, as Henry Green, of the modernist novels *Living*, *Loving* and *Party Going*) and his wife Dig; the witty, opinionated Constant Lambert, composer of *The Rio Grande* and further jazz-inflected ballet scores; and Stephen Spender, already a celebrated poet and communist. The twins, too, became habituées of the Café Royal and David Tennant's Gargoyle Club in Dean Street, epicentres of London's bohemian scene, and Celia's accounts of a typical evening with their extensive circle – drinks here, dinner there, more drinks somewhere else, often rounded off with a late supper of steak and onions at the Savoy Grill – would tax the stamina of the most determined hedonist.

It soon became clear to Mamaine, however, that no affair with Dick could ever be straightforward. However powerful the attraction between them, he had his demons, and she was also, unsurprisingly, highly strung and often neurotic. The first war had scarred Dick permanently, though his courage and natural brio had brought him through it, while the twins had been traumatised by losing both parents and all trace of their happy, settled childhood world. Their fragile health and chronic asthma were a reminder of their deep-seated insecurity. Added to which, Dick was as far from Ging-Ging and Jacko's idea of an acceptable husband for Mamaine as it was possible to be – aside from his wealth, of course. Twenty years her senior, twice married, flamboyantly unconventional, he personified everything that Ging-Ging was doing her level best to protect the twins from – so it was certainly time to move on.

CHAPTER 4

FREEDOM

In September 1937, on their twenty-first birthday, the twins came into the legacy left for them by their father, and they used it to buy a studio house just off the Fulham Road at 102a Drayton Gardens and strike out on their own in a determined bid for independence. They remained deeply devoted to their aunt Ging-Ging and their cousins Wynnie and Anne, who had become like sisters to them. But the imperative to break away from the stultifying, moneyed world of Ibstock Place overcame all lingering scruples about family ties – and certainly no tears were shed at escaping the clutches of Jacko, who was becoming more unpredictable by the day. Celia and Mamaine took grateful possession of their new home, installed bookcases which quickly filled up with the works of their new friends and acquaintances and a grand piano on which they practised enthusiastically, and started creating a comfortable and colourful lair that was much-frequented by their growing circle.

Though the twins were no longer debutantes, the press kept them in their sights, as in this fawning article from *The Sketch* in July 1938:

*Is it Mamaine or is it Celia? One of the Paget twins in the
garden of her Chelsea house.*

The Paget Twins greet you in their barn-house.

A bird's-eye view of the "Twinnies" in their studio taken from the gallery.

The Twins love reading and have a good collection of books.

THE "TWINNIES"
AND THEIR TWIN APARTMENTS.

Now that they have attained their majority and feel really grown up, the Paget
twins, daughters of the late Eric Morton Paget, have taken a little house in
Chelsea, which consists of a large studio with a gallery running alongside,
and twin suites of rooms at either end. They make the studio their living-
room, and it is comfortably furnished without any exaggerations in the way of
style. The Twins' name for each other is "Twinny."

PHOTOGRAPHS BY JANE HAYDON.

Mamaine in a fabulous frock, by
Maggie Rouff, for Harrods

With an independent base in Chelsea and a small private income, they were now free to forge new friendships, to travel wherever the spirit took them, and to enjoy their new-found liberty to the full. People were fascinated by their extraordinary likeness to one another and near-perfect telepathy, and they were often in demand as models for society photographers, Norman Parkinson and Yevonde among them. They did a bit of modelling for Harrods and various fashion houses like Jaeger, as both were effortlessly chic and appreciated the lovely dresses and shoes that modelling brought as its rewards.

Any of the ungainliness of childhood had melted away, leaving them astonishingly pretty and still hard to tell apart at first glance. Although they no longer dressed identically, they often chose similar clothes from their favourite designers, or swapped clothes for particular occasions, sharing their taste in fashion as in so much else. They were sometimes tempted to test their friends' credulity by impersonating one another for the sheer fun of it, seeing how far they could spin the deception out before being rumbled. Quite far, as it turned out – even Sartre was hoodwinked by Celia pretending to be Mamaine on a later trip to Paris.

They travelled as often as they could to the continent, keeping up with the wide circle of friends they had acquired during their spells in Switzerland and Italy. Mamaine's photo album contains snaps of a dizzying range of destinations – Corsica, Crete, Tangiers, Marseilles, Budapest, Salzburg – often taken with friends – bright-eyed, handsome, hopeful, young – who have disappeared into the mists of time, or were to lose their lives in the war. Given their precarious health, the twins made for the cool, dry air of the Alps whenever they could, Kitzbuhel being a favourite spot, and they returned again and again to their favourite *pension* in the Bavarian Alps, where they made new friends on every visit.

Haus Hirth was owned and run with warmth and charm by Johanna Hirth and her second husband, known to all as Onkel Walter. Tante Johanna, as the twins called her, dressed in traditional Austrian dirndls and embroidered blouses, but despite her unassuming appearance she was a woman of innate distinction and her guesthouse was supremely civilised.

She loved the company of artists, musicians and writers, and they gravitated to Haus Hirth from all over the world, creating an atmosphere of intense conviviality and mild suspense, for one never knew who would be sitting at the dinner table the next night. In 1938, one of the twins' companions there was a lively emerald-eyed American called Eleanor Stone, who was immediately struck by their flair, describing them as the two most attractive women she had ever known.

Eleanor, witty, adventurous and a bluestocking, had recently married an impoverished Hungarian baron, Zsigmond Perényi, and moved to his family's small

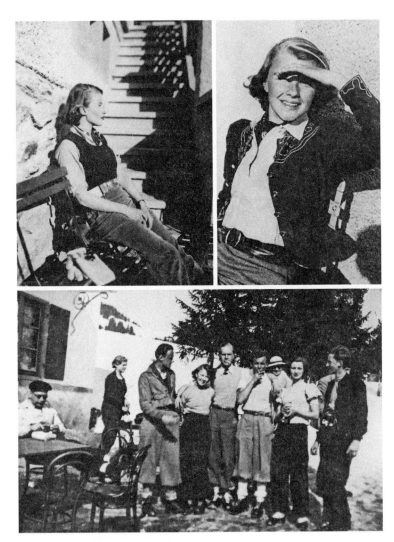

In Kitzbuhel. Mamaine (top left) and Celia (top right)
and below, Celia (second from left) with friends

The Perényis' castle at Szőllős

Baroque castle and estate in Ruthenia, at the edge of the Carpathians. With its pastures, vineyards and forests on the slopes above the castle, it comprised a small feudal world largely dictated by traditional customs and a centuries-old reverence for the nobility. In her memoir *More Was Lost,* Eleanor described her married life at Szőllős with Zsiga, working to drag the old castle – with its frescoed halls, dusty basement and cast of old retainers – into the twentieth century, and forging friendships with a singular circle of local magyars and merchants. Her richly detailed account conjures the now lost world of *mitteleuropa*, poised on the edge of unforeseeable change. Land grabs and border changes had resulted in the estate now being technically in Czechoslovakia, just over the border from Zsiga's native Hungary, and particularly vulnerable to Germany's territorial ambitions. But, although there was acute tension in the air in the summer of 1938, hope that this might be diffused by Chamberlain's forthcoming visit to Munich lingered on.

Zsiga and Eleanor Perényi

That August, as Eleanor reported in *More Was Lost*, 'Celia and Mamaine Paget wrote that they were coming to visit me. They always went abroad in August, and found it entirely natural to make the long, and by now possibly dangerous, trip from England to visit me. "Chamberlain doesn't want a war," they said, "and we aren't ready for it."' She continued:

They were the perfect guests. […] They spent the morning practising Mozart on the piano, and answering letters. They had an active correspondence with at least a hundred people. Our own post swelled with letters from their friends, who were with equal calm vacationing in France, and Italy. We met in the afternoon. We drove them all over the countryside. Zsiga, like so many Central Europeans, had a passion for water. […] So we would go and find little streams and bathe in the hot August afternoons.[8]

The twins stayed for three weeks, growing increasingly fond of Zsiga and he of them. Eleanor liked to quote Celia remarking: '"He has one of the qualities of real genius. One always finds it in the Russian novels. It is that ability to be

Wild swimming in the afternoons

so utterly natural and at the same time profound that if you don't understand such people, you sometimes think them simple.'"

Eleanor then accompanied them to Prague, where they looked up various acquaintances, all of whom seemed strangely unconcerned by the rumours of war. Even the twins' contact at the British Legation was 'vague and insouciant to the last degree'. The height of his outrage seemed to be provoked by the recent visit of Unity Mitford. "'Fancy her running after that dreadful little fellow,'" he remarked over dry martinis served without ice, but he had no real answers to all their questions, so 'the twins sailed coolly off to Germany the next day, and I returned to Zsiga'. This throwaway remark by Eleanor, and her brief description of the twins' stay, underlines how effortlessly they still moved around Europe in the summer of 1938, and how blinkered wide swathes even of Central Europe seemed to be to the conflagration to come. The fact that martinis could be served without ice struck the one ominous note in her account.

Any tenuously held optimism that Hitler's aggression could somehow be diffused was to be proved naive at best, as the faint rumblings of war crescendoed into the thunderous beat of goose-stepping storm-troopers. Naturally, the outbreak of war changed everything. Dick Wyndham was already an army captain, and he joined up in the King's Royal Rifles as soon as war was declared, although he was by now too old for active service.

Promoted to major, he was intermittently transferred around the country with his regiment, and opportunities to meet Mamaine grew few and far between. He tried to persuade her to go along with him, but she was determined to join the war effort herself and do something useful at last.

Without other skills to offer, both she and Celia signed up for nursing duties, and were sent to different hospitals: Mamaine to Warley Woods in Brentwood, and Celia to a base hospital in Chertsey. For

Major Dick Wyndham

some extraordinary reason even this was considered news-worthy enough for the *Weekly Dispatch* of 14 January 1940 to report, under the heading 'Took the War to Part Them' alongside a blurred photo of the twins digging in a field:

> They wear the same uniform of course, just as for 23 years they wore the same kind of clothes, the same kind of hair-bow, the same kind of hair.
>
> But there are no more tricks on chance acquain-tances, no more hoaxing of dance partners, no more practical jokes over a doubtful identity.
>
> War is a serious business and they are keen on their work.
>
> When Christmas was over in their hospitals, the girls met again after three months' separation. They had the same idea about what they wanted to do. Arm in arm, they went off to dig the cabbage patch. [9]

After a few months of 'phoney war' the bombing raids started in earnest, and they decided that if they were to be killed they would prefer to be killed together, so Celia managed to transfer to Warley Woods, where they worked together on the wards, patching soldiers up as best they could through the Blitz and random bombing raids. Despite their own fragility, their nursing bred in them both a steel and resilience they would always draw on, and the camaraderie with other nurses from all walks of life made the labour bearable, however grimly distressing.

Then back, in 1942, to their London base in Drayton Gardens, South Kensington. While they were away nursing they had lent the flat to Cyril Connolly and Peter Quennell, and it had become an outpost for *Horizon* and a hub for the twins' London circle, which comprised all those touched by the journal's widening ripples of influence. Connolly's colleague at *Horizon,* Stephen Spender, even chose Drayton Gardens as the venue for his second wedding, to the pianist Natasha Litvin in April 1941, with Guy Burgess, the poet Louis MacNeice, and the philosopher A. J. Ayer among the guests. Celia and Mamaine had virtually to prise the house back from their tenants.

Celia now joined the revolving merry-go-round that staffed *Horizon*'s offices in Lansdowne Terrace, working as one of several secretaries-cum-editorial-assistants-cum -readers-cum-friends of Cyril's and generally holding the fort until Connolly made his belated appearance around noon. It was a makeshift arrangement, relying on who- ever happened to be available, and in addition to Celia the roster included the writer Anna Kavan, Spender's boy- friend Tony Hyndman, and Connolly's girlfriend Diana Witherby, who struck up a close and lifelong friend- ship with Celia. From time to time, they were joined by Humphrey Slater's girlfriend Janetta Woolley, who breezed in barefoot, bringing with her a strong whiff of bohemia and earning herself the nickname 'Miss Bluefeet', and a 'very ornamental' young man called Michael Nelson, to whom *Horizon*'s angel investor Peter Watson inevitably took a shine. Later, the office settled into more of a routine, and, when Lys Lubbock replaced Diana in Connolly's affections, she joined the glamor- ous and leonine Sonia Brownell in a more executive and permanent role.

Celia

The frenetic and provisional atmosphere of wartime London pervaded every aspect of life, rendering nothing predictable, everything conditional. Friends and lovers would be suddenly called up and would disappear for months or years, their destination uncertain, their fate unknown; others would return from combat wounded, traumatised, or simply changed by forces beyond their control. In such a precarious atmosphere it is perhaps not surprising that Celia broke with her familiar *Horizon* circle to make a hasty and impulsive marriage to a superficially charming Irish screenwriter called Patrick Kirwan, who was handsome, amusing, seventeen years her senior and, as she was to discover too late, far too fond of the bottle. Indeed, his life revolved principally around the pub, where he would pass endless hours with his circle of Irish writers or would-be writers, until they were all too plastered to make any sense at all.

It was a typical Blitz marriage, contracted in haste, doomed to failure, and it inevitably ended in separation after a couple of years. Her cousin Anne realised the writing was on the wall when she picked her way through the bombed-out streets to have supper with Celia and her new husband, only to find him passed out cold, dead drunk, in front of the door to their flat. She was astonished when Celia casually directed Anne to step over the comatose body, leaving him where he was for the rest of the evening while they dined inside, but it was simply par for the course, Celia told her: he was often hopelessly drunk, even if kind and charming when sober. Looking back, Celia was astonished at her impulsiveness; she had never really loved Kirwan, and she loathed the maudlin evenings they spent in pubs with his Irish writer friends in various stages of inebriation. But in the feverish glow of the nightly raids, the fear and the fires and the wanton destruction of war, many put the future on hold and fell in with strange bedfellows.

Mamaine had landed a job working for the Ministry of Economic Warfare, where she stayed in various roles till the end of the war. The MEW was established in the late 1930s to hobble the Axis powers' economies, either by directly interfering with German industrial production and food supply, or, indirectly, by lowering German morale through propaganda and other means, including sabotage; the Special Operations Executive was established in 1940 under the aegis of the MEW, though it soon gained operational independence. The MEW was a large and many-fingered ministry, with intelligence and propaganda a large part of its remit, and with 1,500 staff at its height of operations. Mamaine's job principally

involved doing research for the classicist and Fellow of
Magdalen College, Oxford, C. E. 'Tom Brown' Stevens,
who specialised in 'black' propaganda, producing a series
of German-language newspapers to be dropped into occupied Europe, and broadcasts for German U-boat crews.
It was he who suggested the use of the first four notes of
Beethoven's Symphony No. 5 (which happened also to
spell V for Victory in Morse code) to announce Allied
broadcasts.

Mamaine was still conducting her volatile, long-range
affair with Dick Wyndham, who was now posted to bar-
racks near St Ives in Cornwall where, being a painter, he
naturally gravitated into the circle of Ben and Barbara
Nicholson, Adrian Stokes and Margaret Mellis, then living
in Carbis Bay. Mamaine made a few sorties there by train,
but for months on end it was difficult if not impossible
to meet. I only have his letters to her, suffused with love
and passion but also fraught with anxiety: for neither of
them was the relationship emotionally straightforward.
He wrote to 'My beloved Twinkie' in 1941, after spending
his leave with her, that he longed to marry her, that after
five years 'you have done more than create a love; you have
succeeded, like Frankenstein, in creating a new human
being: a loving old monster known as "good old Dickie"
[…] who feels strange and lonely and utterly dependant
on his creator – Twinks.' He continued, 'For I love you
so much, my darling one – perhaps too much; I am still
confused as to whether you <u>want</u> me to go on loving you
or not: whether you want to love me or not?' And, on
the brink of being posted away for another six months,
he urged her to take the greatest care of herself 'both in

raids and in health' for 'I <u>know</u> we will be eternally happy together; I <u>know</u> we will never be happy apart.'

The seesaw between elation and despair was constant: Mamaine still felt unable to give Dick the undying love he craved. Despite all they shared and their powerful mutual attraction, the strength of his passion often alarmed her, and she struggled to meet it halfway. 'For God's sake, darling,' he urged, 'don't start again the old gag that if I feel so strongly it is better we should not risk a marriage that may fail. That is <u>my</u> risk. It won't fail; and in any case I would rather be with you for five years – even six months – than sacrifice any time of our lives together. [...] And you will know by now that you could never find any other man who could love you as I do.'

Nevertheless, in 1943, Dick, ever restless, left the army and was sent to Beirut as a reporter and 'political observer' for the *News of the World* (a very different paper in those days) and later the *Sunday Times*: roles that fulfilled his love of travel and action, but inevitably separated him from Mamaine for even longer stretches of time. Lebanon was his base, for the time being, but he flew all over the Middle East, from Damascus to Kurdistan to Cairo, reporting on the raids, riots and bombardments, and earning a recommendation that he should be 'awarded a decoration in recognition of my fight for freedom and democracy'. He was torn between the compulsion to cover this particular theatre of conflict and the longing to return to his beloved Tickerage and Mamaine, but the former won. 'I remember you once said that it was extraordinary that at heart my character was good when all my views on life were amoral,' he wrote to Mamaine. 'Only now I begin to

Mamaine at Tickerage

understand what you meant.' He stayed out there, moving to Aleppo and Baghdad, then back to Cairo, writing
voluminous and vivid letters home to Mamaine about his
adventures – which included an expedition among the
Marsh Arabs with the war artist Edward Bawden – and
always wishing he could share them with her. Nevertheless,

his commitments in the Middle East were open-ended, and there was a tacit understanding that each should be free to pursue other entanglements, given his long absences.

I have often speculated on why Mamaine resisted any commitment to Dick, when he pressed her so ardently to marry him. After all, the affair occupied much of her twenties, and she continued to love him and feel for him long after they parted. He had opened her eyes – and Celia's – to another way of living, had enveloped her in culture and beauty, had shaped many of her tastes and desires. The twins often repaired to Tickerage, separately and together, even during Dick's long absences: it had become their haven, too, from the pressures and anxieties of war-torn London.

I shall never know the truth of it, but I suspect that Dick's buccaneering nature threatened to overwhelm Mamaine, and, after all, he held all the cards: wealth and status, age and experience. Added to which, he relished his freedom, and was accustomed to getting his own way. His bouts of domesticity at Tickerage, however idyllic, were merely intervals in his roving, devil-may-care progress through life, in which he courted peril at every turn. For all that, my mother always spoke of him with affection and admiration: for his generosity, his courage, his debonair contempt for convention and full-throated embrace of life. However, as the war staggered into its fourth year and Mamaine's relations with Dick seemed more uncertain than ever, she was to meet someone who would make an even greater claim on her heart.

CHAPTER 5

A CHEQUERED AFFAIR

Mamaine met Arthur Koestler at a party thrown by
Cyril Connolly in January 1944. Koestler, a mercurial
Hungarian-born writer and journalist, was, at the time,
best-known in Britain as the author of the celebrated
Darkness at Noon, his chilling fictionalised exposé of
Stalin's show trials of the late 1930s (translated into English
by his then-girlfriend, Daphne Hardy). More recently he
had published *Arrival and Departure*, a novel that dealt
graphically with the fate of the Jews in Germany, drawing on the testimony of a Polish resistance fighter, Jan
Karski, who had infiltrated Belsen concentration camp and
seen the reality of the Final Solution at first hand. Despite
the fact that the Foreign Secretary Anthony Eden had
informed the House of Commons on 17 December 1942
that the Germans were 'now carrying into effect Hitler's
oft-repeated intention to exterminate the Jewish people
in Europe', a message that caused the House to stand in
silence at the gravity of what it had just heard, the Allied
powers still did not grasp the enormity of the unfolding
genocide, nor fully understand the means by which it was
being achieved.[10]

Koestler was the first to break cover with this story, and when an advance chapter from *Arrival and Departure* describing the 'mixed transports' of cattle trains to the camps was published in the October 1943 issue of *Horizon*, it caused a furore. Many applauded Koestler's courage in revealing what the government had not yet formally acknowledged, but the conservative establishment was swift to cast doubt on his sources, revealing a smouldering anti-Semitism and a blind denial of the irrefutable facts. It was typical of Koestler to challenge the prevailing consensus: he spent his life going against the grain, saying the unsayable, and this, combined with his pugilistic manner, made him as many enemies as friends over the course of a long life animated (or dogged) by controversy.

He was nearly forty and had lived more lives than most people would manage in ninety years. Born in Budapest in 1905 to affluent Jewish parents, he had moved with his family to Vienna when he was nine. During his student years there he became a convinced Zionist and abandoned his studies to join a kibbutz in Palestine. This didn't work out, but he soon found employment as Middle East correspondent for the powerful Ullstein Press, based in Berlin. Arriving in

Arthur Koestler in the early 1940s

Germany in 1930, he was struck by how broken the country was, on the brink of its fall to National Socialism, and
discovered in Marxism the only ideology that he trusted to
counter Nazism. It was a blinding conversion, almost spir-
itual in nature. The Communist Party obligingly commissioned him to travel extensively in the USSR and to record
what he saw; so blinkered was he by his new faith that he
failed to register the horrors of the Ukrainian famine of
1932–33 or the early show trials in Soviet Central Asia.

Returning to Paris (Hitler was, by now, in power in
Berlin) he continued the fight against fascism as best as he
could – editing an émigré journal, activating and raising
funds – before being sent, in 1936, by the *News Chronicle*
to cover the Spanish Civil War, from where he reported
on the extent of Axis support for Franco. When Málaga
fell in 1937 he was arrested by Franco's military intelligence and jailed in Seville, spending ninety-five days in
prison, mainly in solitary confinement, haunted by the
howls and whimpers of fellow prisoners on either side of his
cell as they were dragged daily to their executions. He was
convinced that as a Communist who had testified against
Franco his turn would come at any moment. He was,
instead, sprung from jail in a prisoner exchange, thanks
to international pressure and the machinations of his first
wife, Dorothy Ascher. He recorded the entire horrifying
episode in his book *Dialogue with Death.*

By this time, Koestler's faith in communism was shattered: its manifest dishonesty and misuse of language had
finally penetrated his carapace of denial as news filtered
in of the abuse of principles and imprisonment of friends
throughout the Soviet empire. He resigned his membership

Arthur Koestler in the early 1940s

of the Party in 1938, just as he started work on the devastating novel about the Soviet show trials that would
become *Darkness at Noon*. In Paris, at the outbreak of war,
he was arrested again as an 'enemy alien' and transported
to the verminous and appalling French concentration camp
of Le Vernet in the foothills of the Pyrenees. On release, he
managed to outwit the Nazis and join the Foreign Legion,

and eventually made his way to Britain with false papers, only to be thrown into Pentonville prison as an 'enemy alien' until his identity could be ascertained. The high-wire cat-and-mouse game he played (and won) with the Nazis in the early years of war was the subject of his first book written in English, *Scum of the Earth,* which he composed while lecturing for the Army, driving ambulances, and working for the Ministry of Information, writing propaganda films and leaflets to be dropped over Germany. He also produced radio essays and broadcasts for the BBC, and a string of trenchant articles for *Horizon* and other papers and magazines in Britain and America.

In person, he was articulate (albeit with a strong and ineradicable Hungarian accent), opinionated, intense and attractive, dark and of medium height with a pointed face and restless, mobile features. He had recently parted from his girlfriend Daphne, after a six-year affair, but was not yet reconciled to the fact and was, consequently, in a despondent frame of mind. Mamaine's affair with Dick Wyndham had all but petered out, thanks to Dick's long absences from England; she therefore considered herself free, but in no hurry to find another lover. At twenty-eight she was strikingly beautiful, with a droll and often flippant turn of phrase that kept her more importunate admirers at bay. She, too, at this point, felt insecure and unsatisfied with her lot, longing to find more rewarding work than her current job at the Ministry of Economic Warfare, and a firmer basis for her future life.

The attraction was far from immediate. Arthur found Mamaine distant – even aloof – at first, but her appearance and archness of manner appealed to him nevertheless, and he soon dubbed her 'Mermaid' in his diary. It took several more chance meetings and dinners before the frost fully thawed and Arthur could report in his diary, 'dinner and uneasy seduction of Mermaid'. It was an attraction of opposites in so many ways, charged with contradictions, which proved both its strength and its fatal weakness. Arthur was the quintessential European, deracinated, almost stateless, a Jewish firebrand, while Mamaine was the product of generations of English gentry, and deeply rooted in British life and culture, however restless the war had made her. But, against the prevailing chaos of conflict, neither felt strongly grounded, and neither was satisfied with their current situation. They shared many friends and acquaintances in the intellectual world, a keen sense of humour and liberal instincts. Nevertheless, Arthur's volatility and Mamaine's febrile sensibility made for a heady cocktail.

During the summer of 1944 their relationship developed into one of passionate encounters and bitter rows, and Arthur found himself falling in love – but not without misgivings. Riven with neurotic hang-ups of various sorts, of which he was fully aware yet incapable of conquering, he could not even contemplate a simple love affair without ambiguity or strife. Mamaine's relative equanimity was tested to the limits by his unreasonable demands, his tempestuous moods, his drinking and his self-denying ordinances. While longing for her, he frequently lashed out at her verbally; he could be irritable, impatient and morose. But her defiance was a good foil to Koestler's overbearing manner and kept her inoculated against his wilder mood swings; and when he wasn't tortured by writer's block or seething with resentment against his political opponents, she found him an irresistible companion and admired his unequivocal and forcefully held convictions.

He had more vitality than anyone she had ever met, a quicksilver wit allied to a deep seriousness of purpose, and the *savoir faire* of a man who had already lived life to the hilt. Soon she was calling him, teasingly, 'the sage AK'. She was constantly amused by his comic semi-mastery of the English language – there was a (possibly apocryphal) story of Arthur, newly arrived in England, backing like a scalded cat out of a public telephone box after reading the instruction (as he thought) to 'Please put your penis in the slot'. Unpredictable, cosmopolitan, his behaviour so at odds with the English rectitude with which she was familiar, Arthur offered a bracing novelty and a challenge to Mamaine, who always rose to a challenge. The affair swiftly took on an importance for her that she had not felt since breaking up with Dick Wyndham; she fell in love with Koestler the writer and thinker as much as Koestler the man. Eleven years her senior, he also fulfilled (again) her subliminal desire for a relationship with an older man.

Their chequered affair tentatively survived an eight-month separation from Christmas 1944 when Arthur was posted to Palestine, ostensibly as a correspondent for *The Times,* though in fact on a secret mission to win the Palestinians over to partition. While apart, they corresponded as intimately as the censors would allow, under the code names 'Nyuszi/Uncle Arthur' and 'Mermaid'. On 31 December Mamaine wrote:

My darling Nyuszi, Thankyou for your sweet letter from the boat. Getting it was the nicest thing that has happened to me since you went away. Christmas was not much fun as Celia got ill, so I brought her here & looked after her in the intervals of sitting in an icy office. She is now in a nursing home in Highgate which is also a convent. She has had a bad time but is getting on all right (collapse of the lung – pleurisy). [...] It was bloody awful when you went away – you were so incredibly sweet to me and made me so very happy, that is why I was so miserable when you left. [...] I am afraid Celia being ill will make it difficult for me to leave my job. I don't see how she can be back at work before the middle of February.

Mamaine was tired of London without Arthur's bracing presence, and determined to leave her unrewarding desk

Mamaine

job and, if possible, get posted abroad. In January 1945 she wrote:

> Ever since you left I have been engaged in absolutely feverish manoeuvrings to get myself a job in Paris, but though I have lunched with quite influential people and dined with them too (bringing up all the funds of my sex-appeal, such as it is) I simply cannot get anybody to say anything definite. They all seem quite willing to give me jobs, but say either that they don't know what jobs they have, or that it is almost impossible to export people, or something like that. I even tried some 'scene-shifting' at the MOI to get to Baghdad or Beyrout or Teheran; here too I pulled strings like Harpo Marx on the night of the opera, but to no avail […]

That same month Koestler made the decision to rent an old farmhouse in the wilds of Snowdonia called Bwlch Ocyn. They had found it together the previous summer, and he asked Mamaine to oversee the repairs and arrangements for him. It was far from the temptations of London, and therefore a perfect place to focus on the writing he planned on his return. She wrote to tell him how pleased she was: 'it is such a lovely house, you will be able to live there most of the time & then nearly all your problems will be solved. I would like to live there with you if you weren't such a Branch Street Kid, but anyway I will come and stay with you perhaps and cook you lovely post-war meals.'

In February she wrote more cheerfully, relieved at Celia's recovery:

So glad you are in such a beautiful place and having a lovely time – I'm envious, it's cold and grey and dismal here. I never go out at night at all, but I don't mind because my morale is very good and I never get *cafards* and don't feel bored either.* The only thing I suffer from is having too much energy and not enough to do with it. For my health is now so extravagantly good and I sleep so well and eat such a lot that I could work 12 hours a day if only I had enough work. […] [L]ast time I wrote to you I thought the war would never end, but now I think it will quite soon; so of course the whole outlook has changed for me and I feel much more cheerful and optimistic. All hope is not dead in my bosom […] What else can I say? You are impossible to write to because (unlike most men) you understand everything so well that there seems no need to say it at all . . .

PS Please note my name is spelt MAMAINE; write it out 100 times. Dick [Wyndham] is in Cairo and I think he must be coming back soon. Did I tell you that I am learning Turkish on the principle (instilled in me by you) that 'it may come in handy sometime'? The Turkish govt. gives free lessons; I go to them. Saw Cyril the other day, just back from Paris where he stayed at the Embassy. Said he hadn't had one bad meal, the only time complaints were made was when there wasn't any salad with the foie gras!!

---

* 'depressions'

Arthur replied from Palestine:

> Darling, I have just come back from Galilee and
> found your letter. I love your letters, everybody else
> writes me about politics and highfalutin' matters, but
> each line of yours makes me homesick for London.
> When I came out I toyed with the idea of perhaps
> settling here; after a month I find that I love this
> country more than I ever thought – the incredible
> beauty of the landscape more than anything else –
> but that living here would mean to abdicate as a
> writer. The people here are so obsessed with their own
> tragedy and the problems of the country that Europe
> becomes very remote and within a few months they
> lose touch; it is an inevitable process […] But the
> main obstacle is the language question; my English is
> (as you know) a very tender plant which would soon
> dry up in a foreign environment […].

They continued to discuss, in an entirely open-ended way,
Arthur's plan to settle in Wales on his return, ideally with
Mamaine. Neither wanted to make too many demands
on the other, and both were still wary of commitment.
'[…] this house is a kind of common enterprise of ours,'
Arthur wrote, 'and I can't imagine moving in without
you, at least for the first few weeks. Anyway, September
would be just the right time and it would be terrible fun
to shift the furniture about together. Should you by then
have developed – how does one say it without shocking the
censor – other ties, I shall nevertheless kidnap you for a
few weeks.'

Mamaine was approached by the Ministry of Information about a job with the press attaché in Jerusalem, which she would have leapt at, as she longed to experience life in Palestine, but to her frustration it never materialised. 'JOB FALLEN THROUGH CAN'T STICK THIS COUNTRY ANY LONGER STOP CAN YOU OR DICK DO ANYTHING LOVE PAGET,' she wired Arthur, following up with, 'Darling Nyuszi, isn't it sad my Palestine job has fallen through […] You see I don't want to stay in England. I can't bear it any longer; & all the jobs I've been offered mean working in London so I don't want them. God you are lucky to be free; I shan't be until the end of the Japanese war.' However, she had a more important bone to pick: she was still closely in touch with Dick Wyndham, and knew that he and Arthur met occasionally to argue politics and – bitter rivals as they were for her affections – to discuss her. 'I had a letter from Dick from Jerusalem, rather depressed as a result, apparently, of dining with you. You might be a bit more considerate: you know that if I met Daphne I would rather cut my tongue out than say anything about you & me which might possibly depress her.'

Dick was still struggling to come to terms with Mamaine's affair with Arthur, and his latest letter had deeply unsettled her. He wrote of how she had made him

homesick again for Tick, and lovesick all over again for you, when I started remembering music, and the ducks, and our walks to hear the nightingales, your sweet paintings, and the piano scales from across the lake. What troubles me when I get into this

mood is whether I can ever be really happy there
without you (any more than I could be comfortable
without electricity and coal, and the water cut off),
because when I was not noticing it so much before
the war you became a part of everything there – and
my life.

She still cared for him, too, and found his suffering on her
account hard to countenance.

In April 1945 with Arthur still away, a third admirer
turned up in London in the unlikely form of the American
man of letters Edmund Wilson. Aged fifty, Wilson was at
the height of his reputation: his 1931 collection of literary
essays *Axel's Castle* had established him as an impressive
literary voice, and his journalism in the *New Yorker* and
New Republic consolidated his reputation as America's chief
critic and literary arbiter. He wrote about ideas as well as
books: in *To the Finland Station* (1940), his exploration
of the intellectual roots of socialism and communism, he
set out his stall against Marxism and its more egregious
failings, making clear that he never had any illusions about
Stalin. In this, he aligned himself instantly with Koestler,
Orwell and other writers of the liberal Left.

Wilson was nominally still married to the celebrated
writer and critic Mary McCarthy, fifteen years his junior
and mother of their son Reuel, but their marriage had
staled, and he was never able to resist an attractive woman.
He now found himself captivated by Mamaine, whom he
proceeded to court with a persistence that earned him her
undying friendship, if not her love.

CHAPTER 6

THE RIVAL

'Edmund Wilson the American writer has been over here on his way to Italy,' Mamaine wrote to Arthur, perhaps to punish him for his tactlessness with Dick.

> I met him dining with Rodney Phillips, Humphrey Slater and John Strachey and after that I saw a lot of him until he went. We used to sit up very late talking because he was supposed to be leaving the next day, and it kept being put off so we had to do it several times. He is rather shy and dull at first but improves a lot when one gets to know him and I think he has quite a lot of bright ideas though he is not nearly as good at saying them as you are; but he doesn't brow-beat me the way you do either, and doesn't mind telling me about things I want to know about. [...] Do you think he is a good writer? I have never read anything by him except *Axel's Castle*, but he says *To the Finland Station* is much better [...].

On some of their long evenings together, she and Edmund walked through the wartime streets of London, and she took him to the first night of Britten's opera *Peter Grimes* at Sadlers Wells, which fascinated him. Wilson wrote the opera up later, alongside a more detailed sketch of Mamaine, in *Europe without Baedeker*. 'Do get Edmund's book *Europe without Baedeker* and read about me,' she wrote to Celia in 1947 when the book came out. 'Unfortunately it is a bad book so

Edmund Wilson

my immortality is not assured; but perhaps that is after all just as well, particularly as he very clearly hints that I was his mistress, which God forbid! I am called "G".'

In it, Wilson describes Mamaine's attractions and contradictions:

> along with her matter-of-factness, a volatility of mood and expression that always enchants me in women; the beauty that seems to derive from a spirit which inhabits a body rather than from the body itself. This spirit, in G., sleeps or wakes, fades or flushes, is *méchant* or merry, flits about through a repertory of several roles, and has its moments of strength and of weakness. Sometimes she looks frightened or a little out of focus, with the two sides of her face not in harmony: one pert, the other chagrined; sometimes on guard and alert, like a keen-

ARIANE BANKES

eyed quiet baby fox that makes quick silent darting
movements; sometimes lovely with delicate colour-
ing or electric with the kind of intensity in which
feeling and intellect mix.[11]

He comments on her beautiful handwriting 'with its dis-
tinctly detached letters, its deftly twisted ampersands and
its incised serifs and shadings', which he said matched a
curiously formal turn of phrase alongside a 'crisp schoolboy code that makes everything matter-of-fact and droll',
typical of English girls. As he confessed to a friend later,
'I fell terribly in love in London with a young English
girl – twenty-seven [Mamaine was, in fact, twenty-nine]
and one of the brightest I have ever known and – need I
say? – rather neurotic. We talked about getting married
and she was trying to join me in Italy […] I haven't been
so upset since my youth.' Wilson was twenty-one years
older than Mamaine, and he did admit, 'I suppose, after
my experience with Mary [McCarthy, his now estranged
wife] I've been a lunatic to think of getting married to an
even younger girl,' but he was hopelessly and poignantly
in love.[12]

Tactfully rebuffed by Mamaine, he returned to the
States, and a lively correspondence got underway. 'I miss
you a lot,' she wrote, 'nobody I know here is half as much
fun to be with as you.' Perhaps encouraged by this, he
proposed marriage in late May: 'I've never felt a natural
understanding with any woman come so quickly as it has
with you, and the month that I've been away from you,
instead of diminishing my desire for you and this feeling
of understanding, has made them stronger and stronger.'

More pragmatically, he continued, 'There are no practical obstacles on my side: I've called Mary suggesting that she get a divorce during the summer.'

That entreaty failing, he flew back to London in June bearing gifts – earrings, silk stockings, a book by her friend Ignazio Silone among them – all of which were welcome in rationed, war-torn London, but Mamaine firmly rejected him, still loyal to Koestler: 'I don't think I can marry you or do anything to make our relationship fit a conventional pattern, if it doesn't do so already.' Licking his wounds, he retreated to Rome, writing to her sadly, 'I still, despite our snapping and snarlings in London, feel closer to you than I do to anybody else (perhaps an illusion).'

The to-ing and fro-ing about marriage continued an unconscionably long time, testimony to Edmund's persistence, at least. Mamaine became one of his most regular correspondents, sending him wry, gossipy letters about the situation in Britain: VE Day, her encounter with newly released prisoners of war, the excitement at the Labour party's victory in the election, Anglo-American relations, which she teasingly claimed were threatened by an anti-British article of Edmund's in the

Mamaine

Mamaine's letter to Edmund about the VE Day celebrations

New Yorker. The end of war celebrations were, for her, a disappointment:

> . . . in Piccadilly Circus [and] Leicester Square, VE Day seemed a purely American affair. I managed to acquire a sailor's hat made of cardboard with HI YER BABE written on it & a rattle that sounded

like a machine-gun & helped to clear a passage through the crowds. Perhaps after 5½ years of war the English people have forgotten how to enjoy themselves, or perhaps they don't really believe in the peace, or don't see what difference it will make: anyway nobody really got gay yesterday and the whole thing was rather like flat champagne. [...] Somebody brought me some loot from Germany in the form of a book of Hölderlin's letters, captured from an SS HQ. I hope the SS men absorbed some of Hölderlin's views about the Germans before they got captured.

In another letter she reassured Edmund,

Everybody including me misses you very much. I have seen Cyril & Stephen [Spender] – they both said how nice and wonderful you were, only Stephen was rather pained by your *New Yorker* article which he said was <u>terribly</u> anti-British. Last night I dined with Cyril & the famous Sergeant (Stuart Preston), an American who took London by storm a couple of years ago, & who really is an extremely charming, amiable, and cultured young man. The Sergeant was all agog to hear about you. I made mental comparisons of you & him which were entirely to your disadvantage, because the Sergeant likes Europe & doesn't mind what time he has dinner & never says one reminds him of a certain type of American girl. I wish you had been there [...].

The rollercoaster of emotions and the strain of rejecting Wilson's unflagging courtship in favour of the absent and unpredictable Koestler took a toll on Mamaine's health, which always deteriorated under stress, and that summer she was invalided out of her job at the Ministry of Economic Warfare. Arthur managed to get an urgent flight home from Palestine in August 1945 and after a passionate reunion proposed marriage to Mamaine, with the proviso that he would never want children. He subscribed to Cyril Connolly's premise that the 'pram in the hall' would prevent him from serious writing, and he was adamant about that. Mamaine refused to undertake *not* to have children, so they compromised by agreeing to go and live together, unmarried, in Bwlch Ocyn, the Welsh farmhouse that Arthur had found for rent before his departure, and on which Mamaine had been overseeing repairs on his behalf.

When she admitted in a letter to Edmund that Arthur had flatly refused to have children, 'so there seems no chance of getting married and not much point in doing so', Edmund's hopes revived, and he was somewhat mollified about Arthur's iron grip on Mamaine's affections by being told, 'Arthur is a great fan of yours and was very crestfallen when I told him you'd never read any of his books.' Edmund dreamed up a package in which she would come over to the States (which she longed to do), inviting her to 'look the situation over? I could send you the money for the trip and you could repay me by working as my secretary.' It is hardly surprising that she didn't fall for that, so he followed up with an appeal to her more materialist side, offering to 'outfit you at Saks Fifth Avenue' and repeating that they could marry and have the children she so longed

Bwlch Ocyn

for. But no: 'I really thought I had told you I wouldn't marry you, but if not please accept herewith my official refusal,' Mamaine confirmed in an otherwise chatty letter in September 1946 – and that, finally, was that: Edmund was soon to marry Elena Mumm Thornton (of the great champagne marque) instead. His romantic notions may have been dashed, but it was far from the end of Edmund's devotion to Mamaine; he continued to see her whenever possible on his travels to Europe, and they maintained a lively correspondence about books, articles, politics and mutual friends throughout her years with Arthur, and beyond. They met up for the last time in February 1954, in Paris, where they were both staying at the same hotel – only a short while before she succumbed to her final, and fatal, illness.

•

Arthur and Mamaine settled at Bwlch Ocyn in August 1945 with a newly acquired sheepdog puppy and some hens. They would manage to stay put for two years. The house was perched high on the south side of the Vale of Ffestiniog, with the Italianate resort of Portmeirion to the sea side and the grim slate-mining town of Blainau to the north. The Snowdonia mountains, visible from their windows, reminded Arthur of the Austria of his youth, and Mamaine had loved the countryside and craved a life there ever since her childhood in rural Suffolk. A low-slung seventeenth-century farmhouse with thick granite walls, stone flags and a roof of locally quarried slate, Bwlch Ocyn was almost impossible to keep warm and dry during bleak weather – and there was a lot of bleak weather about. That first winter of 1945–46 was a bitter one: the water froze in the lavatory cistern ('"It's been pleasantly cool in the peeing department," as K put it'), and when it snowed the drive was impassable. Nevertheless, they arranged the house as best they could, with small sitting rooms for both Arthur and Mamaine; hers was next to the kitchen, 'so that I can, so to speak, read in it while stirring the stew with one hand. This is most convenient, as you can imagine,' she wrote to Celia, 'even now I am in the middle of cooking an enormous ox's heart, which can be heard sizzling away.'

They initially knew no one in the neighbourhood, but Arthur's love of pubs was satisfied by the proximity of the Oakley Arms a few miles away, where he could while away evenings with the locals when the lure of alcohol and disputation got the better of him. Bwlch Ocyn had once belonged to the family of Clough Williams-Ellis, architect of nearby Portmeirion, who still lived nearby with his wife

Amabel (niece of Lytton Strachey) and had attracted a colony of like-minded people, among them the philosopher Bertrand Russell and his third wife Patricia, always called Peter. Russell was, by then, a world-famous public intellectual, in demand both as a philosopher and mathematician, and as a broadcaster on varied topical subjects and member of *The Brains Trust*. Like Koestler and Orwell, he was deeply pessimistic about the future of peace in a world that contained the atomic bomb. His earlier stance of appeasement had morphed into a more pragmatic 'relative political pacifism', and he was broadly in favour of a Jewish homeland. So, he and Arthur had much in common, but also much to spar about. The scarcity of food under rationing made entertaining rather a perilous activity, however; when the Russells first came to lunch 'we nearly broke our necks trying to get some food for him, as K had invited him just when we had nothing'.

On the rare occasions when Mamaine was not working with Arthur as secretary, scribe or sounding board for new ideas, she was fully occupied in eking out their meagre rations in the kitchen, or in housekeeping, which she loathed. Bit by bit they acquired more creature comforts, including a radiogram to listen to the Third Programme in the evenings. When they got more settled they would have a succession of friends to stay – Celia, George Orwell, the Labour politician Richard Crossman and his wife Zita, the former Free French agent Guy de Rothschild and his wife Alix, the philosopher A. J. (Freddie) Ayer – and would launch occasional raids on London or Paris to top up on social life; otherwise they evolved a largely satisfying routine of hard work and erratic housekeeping, punctuated with occasional flare-ups about which Mamaine was, initially, philosophical: 'Relations with K could not be better, and he has made several encouraging remarks such as that he has never lived so well with anybody else, and that he can't see what can go wrong with our *ménage*. Also he keeps saying how happy he is and we are – isn't it wonderful?' she wrote to Celia soon after their arrival in Wales. Having thrown in her lot with Arthur, Mamaine buried her latent longing for children, and focused on creating as fulfilling a life as she could with him.

CHAPTER 7

THE AFFECTION YOU CAN
FEEL FOR A STRANGER

That Christmas of 1945, their first in the Welsh farmhouse, Mamaine and Arthur decided to invite George Orwell with his baby son Richard to stay, along with Celia. Arthur greatly liked and admired Orwell, whom he regarded as comrade in arms in their mutual campaign to open the eyes of the political Left to the dangers of communism. Koestler and Orwell had first met in 1941, after Orwell had positively reviewed *Darkness at Noon*. At that time, Arthur was finding his feet in literary London through Cyril Connolly's many introductions, and both men were working in wartime propaganda: Orwell for the Indian Service of the BBC and Koestler for the Ministry of Information, where he wrote anti-Nazi broadcasts for the BBC's Home Service, and for the War Office, where he became increasingly expert in cultural propaganda. Orwell had asked Koestler to contribute to a series of pocket-sized volumes called Searchlight Books which he was editing for Secker & Warburg, and which aimed to provide a left-wing rationale for the war against Hitler. Orwell himself contributed the first title, *The Lion and the Unicorn*, but enemy bombing of the printing works combined with paper shortages brought the series to an abrupt end, and Koestler's projected *The Streets of Europe* never took its place beside the dozen other titles.

Koestler and Orwell recognised that they were cut from the same cloth politically, though they were wildly divergent in every other way. Orwell was the sober, diffident English ascetic, while Koestler was the cosmopolitan, hedonistic Hungarian – yet they were united in their conviction about the threat posed by communism to democracy and the rule of law, and the urgent need to do what they could about it. In July 1944, Koestler received a package from Orwell containing the manuscript of *Animal Farm*, which he read with mounting excitement. 'Envious congratulations,' he wrote to Orwell. 'This is a glorious and heart-breaking allegory: it has the poesy of a fairytale and the precision of a chess problem. Reviewers will say it ranks with Swift, and I shall agree with them.'[13]

It would be another year until *Animal Farm* was published: its portrayal of the Soviet leaders as gross and devious pigs was thought by many to be a step too far for a public that had been gently coddled by wartime propaganda into thinking of 'Uncle Joe' Stalin as a cosy ally against the Nazis, his vast crimes swept conveniently under the carpet. Several notable publishers turned the book down – Jonathan Cape on the recommendation of a 'senior official' at the Ministry of Information whom we shall meet

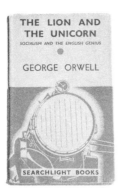

Orwell's volume for
Searchlight Books

later in this story – and, after Fred Warburg finally took the plunge and paid Orwell an advance of £100, paper rationing caused further delays. By the time of *Animal Farm*'s publication in August 1945, however, the West was becoming disabused of its faith in the Soviet regime, and his coruscating fable brought Orwell unprecedented sales and nationwide fame. No longer was he just a respected journalist, broadcaster for the BBC and semi-successful novelist; now he was seen as the conscience of his generation and a brilliant polemicist whose views were sought on almost every subject. On a personal front, however, he was struggling: his wife Eileen had died suddenly during an operation in March, leaving him wretchedly lonely and anxious about how to give their recently adopted son Richard a stable and loving home.

In the autumn Koestler had been in touch with Orwell again about a new proposal, that they should set up together a League for the Dignity and Rights of Man to take the lead in debates about the shape of the post-war world, and 'to defend the individual against the arbitrary action of the state'.[14] Arthur wanted to discuss his ideas for the League in more detail with Orwell, and sketch out a Manifesto to take it forward. This they were to do during the Christmas visit, taking long walks in the hills around Blwch Ocyn, Orwell with Richard cradled on his hip. Celia was to be the other guest.

Celia, at twenty-nine, was now separated from Patrick Kirwan, and seeking a divorce. She had just landed a new job as assistant editor on *Polemic: A Magazine of Philosophy, Psychology and Aesthetics,* an elegant new bi-monthly journal dealing with contemporary thought,

Polemic Issue 1

which was funded by the wealthy publisher Rodney Phillips and edited by the ex-communist, painter and intellectual Humphrey Slater. Orwell's essay 'Notes on Nationalism' had just appeared in the first issue (with a cover designed by Ben Nicholson) alongside articles by Bertrand Russell, A. J. Ayer, Stephen Spender and Henry Miller, and he was to contribute three more essays and an editorial over the two-year life of the magazine.

At this point, Celia and George must have been in touch, presumably through *Polemic*, because she sent Mamaine a note saying, 'Twine, yes, Donkey George O. is coming up for Christmas and we are going to travel up together on Sat the 23rd. Could you possibly meet us at Ruabon? [...] He is bringing his baby (aged 18 months) who he says is not very house-trained but is otherwise easy to cope with. Do you really want me to think of anyone else? – that would make us four, which seems perfect to me.' The twins' nickname for Orwell, Donkey George, was based on Benjamin, the donkey in *Animal Farm* who persists in his stubborn scepticism till the end, but whose certainty that 'life would go on as it had

Polemic Issue 2

always gone on – that is, badly' for the animals proves, of course, to be the ultimate truth.

They met at Paddington Station. As Celia described it later in a BBC radio interview, 'Well, there he was on the platform, easy to recognise, even if you'd never seen him before. A tall, slightly shaggy figure, with his upright brush-like hair, carrying this baby on one arm, and his suitcase in another.' It was a success from the start; Celia was entranced by Richard, getting him to sit next to her on the train and reading him stories, so they had a perfectly happy journey. 'It's difficult to describe what's special about someone,' she continued,

> but I do remember that I was immediately struck by this quality George had. And I was already thinking by the time we were halfway up to Wales, I would really like George and me to become friends. When we got there, George looked after Richard perfectly, as he always did. He used to look after Richard as to the manner born. How he did it I don't know, because he'd never had a baby before. [...] In those days it was very unusual [for a man]. But he really loved doing it, and Richard simply loved George. If George showed any signs of going off without Richard, Richard used to howl, and go on howling until George came back for him.[15]

Later, recalling that journey, she quoted George's own words near the start of *Homage to Catalonia:* 'Queer, the affection you can feel for a stranger!'

Orwell with Richard

Christmas was enlivened by various lunch parties and social events but was not without its strains. Arthur drank so much on Christmas day that he 'more or less passed out over lunch, then woke up and started singing French songs,' Mamaine noted in her diary. 'Meanwhile, George's baby, Richard, aged 19 months, was turning the house upside down, & nearly driving Arthur mad.' Arthur was not fond of babies, indeed he didn't see the point of them at all, so his short fuse was tested to the very limit. Mamaine did, however, record that early one morning Arthur spent an entire hour crouched on the floor making faces at Richard through the bars of his cot to keep him quiet while the exhausted George got some badly needed extra sleep.

George for his part was immediately attracted to Celia and touched by her evident affection for Richard. As she later recalled in the same interview,

Over Christmas we had a game of 'Truth' and a discussion about what qualities one would like to have if you could choose, and George said, 'If I could choose mine, I should like to be irresistible to women,' which was rather a surprise, somehow. I think George liked me very much, because I loved small children, and I loved Richard because he was a very sweet small child. So I think that's what made George feel interested in me. He wanted someone to look after Richard, because he didn't have a wife, you see.

She was perhaps being disingenuous; he was plainly smitten, and found in her a sympathetic and kindred spirit with whom he could discuss ideas, politics and culture on an equal level. Naturally left-wing (she never voted anything but Labour), intellectually curious, lively and kind, she was now at the centre of the intellectual circle that orbited *Polemic*, and she commanded George's respect as well as his affection. She found him amusing and easy to get on with, and appealingly masculine, if not particularly romantic or physically attractive. At any rate, he followed up immediately after their Christmas break with an invitation to visit him in London. He told Celia that he thought he could always tell with twins, even identical twins, which was the older and was sure it was Mamaine; wrong, Celia told him, it was her.

'Shortly after we met,' Celia remembered, 'he invited me round to his flat at 27b Canonbury Square, where he was bathing the baby and putting on his nappy. He was absolutely marvellous with Richard [...]'. After that first visit, she would sometimes return there on a Tuesday, which was Richard's nanny's day off, and help George to entertain Richard, or hold the fort. Islington, even Canonbury Square with its grand Georgian terraces, was bleak in 1946; the pre-war paint was peeling and many of the railings had been commandeered during the war to make munitions. Orwell's third-floor flat was typically austere, with a long draughty corridor that was even colder than it need have been, as none of the doors quite reached the floor and it never occurred to him to put in draught excluders. There was a small room with a workbench where he liked to construct odd bits of furniture and make toys for Richard, none of which were robust enough to last very long.

The only room with a fire was the sitting room – George was no good at housework, but he did love laying fires and managed to keep one in most days despite the fuel rationing – but the flat was otherwise cheerless, with no creature comforts and little decoration. The nanny, Susan Watt, had tried to inject some colour by dyeing the sitting-room curtains red and hanging a print by Douanier Rousseau above the divan bed in which George slept; otherwise, the only colour to catch the eye came from a handful of postcards which hung from a screen. He believed that everyone should live as the working classes did, and seemed oblivious to the fact that they often made their homes as comfortable and cosy as they could, within limited means. He, meanwhile – who could well have afforded it – eschewed any 'luxuries' or new-fangled appliances, even a refrigerator, keeping milk and meat in an icebox. And, ascetic as he was, he kept no wine or spirits in the house.

Orwell was at this point frantically busy, writing all morning, sometimes lunching with friends in Fleet Street and, after nursery tea with Richard, typing into the early hours of the morning to produce a stream of articles for *Tribune*, *Polemic*, the *Observer* and Cyril Connolly's *Horizon*. The idea for a League for the Dignity and Rights of Man, which he and Arthur had discussed over the Christmas visit, was still on the table; Orwell produced a draft manifesto in early January, and Koestler tried but failed to get Bertrand Russell's backing for it, while Orwell attempted to garner support from the journalist Tom Hopkinson, editor of *Picture Post*. Despite both their efforts the project lost momentum and petered out over the ensuing months.

The demands of career, illness, helping friends out where he could and looking after Richard were taking their toll. In order to fit it all in, Orwell lived and worked to a strict and ruthless timetable, governed by the clock. Each evening, before returning to his writing desk, he would have high tea, often sardines, toast and Oxford marmalade with strong black tea, 'as thick as treacle', poured from an immense pot, almost too heavy to lift when full. Indeed, as he wrote in his essay 'A Nice Cup of Tea' for the *Evening Standard* in mid-January 1946, shortly after he met Celia, 'I maintain that one strong cup of tea is better than 20 weak ones.' He went on to enumerate his eleven rules for the perfect cup of tea and, in this as so much else, he was a stickler. It had to be bitter, 'just as beer is meant to be bitter'; sweetening it with sugar was anathema to him. I'm amused to think of Celia, who frankly preferred a gin and tonic to tea of any strength at all, being plied with Orwell's special brew, but she was delighted to lend a hand whenever she could.

A genuine friendship took root and, inevitably but with some diffidence, he proposed. Celia was not the first: he had proposed the previous autumn to Sonia Brownell, siren of *Horizon,* but she had turned him down flat, without hope of reprieve – ironic, in view of her marrying him in late 1949 when he was virtually on his deathbed. Sonia had no feeling for children and shuddered at the memory of George's rooms with their subtle undertow of nappies and cabbage, so far from the elegant literary salons that she dreamed of inhabiting. Later that spring of 1946, he would try his luck again with handsome, clever Olivier Popham, who was grieving her lover, the painter Graham Bell who had died in the war, and was not yet married to Quentin Bell (no relation), younger son of Clive and Vanessa Bell. Olivier was occupying the flat below his in Canonbury Square before embarking for Germany to retrieve artworks sequestered by the Nazis during the war, but the surprise tactics George employed and clumsiness of his approach were guaranteed to fail with her, too.

It was different with Celia, who was genuinely drawn to George, and to Richard, and who saw all they potentially had in common. She soon noticed that George's fingertips were rounded and swollen, which she recognised as a symptom of bronchiectasis, a lung disease in which the airways are widened, leading to a build-up of mucus – a disease from which she herself had suffered. His other symptoms included a persistent phlegmy cough, recurrent infections and, occasionally, coughing up blood. When an infection set in, the only way George could reduce his temperature was by eating nothing but bread. 'It is very awkward for him sometimes, for instance in the Spanish war, and when he was in Germany last summer,' wrote Celia to Mamaine, 'because he has either to live on bread and wine, or have a roaring temperature all the time.'

Such shafts of empathy were common between them. Perhaps he was right, then, not to take her first refusal as final, and to try to win her round, while simultaneously voicing reasons why Celia might be reluctant to marry him – such as the fact that he was fifteen years older than her – presumably in order to shield himself from disappointment. 'He came to lunch on Sunday and asked me again whether I would consider marrying him, or at any rate having an affair with him,' she told Mamaine. Celia was disturbed by talk of an affair 'as he makes it somehow awfully difficult to refuse'. She told George that she was not in love with him, but – even though, as she confided to Mamaine, she thought it was going to be 'more and more difficult to cope with him' – she wanted to continue their friendship. 'What is your advice?' she pleaded.

Celia and Mamaine's own chronic asthma would have made them deeply sympathetic to Orwell's health problems. Ironically, his health at that point was not so much more parlous than Celia's own: she had only recently recovered from a collapsed lung and was to suffer several further crises in the coming years. It was a point of contact, an unspoken bond that cemented their mutual understanding, for chronic ill health places the sufferer in a different register from others and confers on life a sharp and precarious edge.

Another bond was their mutual love of the countryside and their shared affection for Suffolk, where they had both lived when young. Now that they were largely confined to London by work and circumstance, both longed to leave it for a life lived deep in nature, more attuned to the rhythm of the seasons. In the mid-1930s, while married to Eileen, Orwell had made his home in Wallington in Hertfordshire where he tended his roses and milked his goat and took huge pride in the vegetables he managed to grow; he still returned there sporadically whenever his crushing work-load allowed. But Wallington was not wild enough for his tastes, and he was soon to set sail for the remote farm-house called Barnhill on the Isle of Jura. Celia, meanwhile, still pined for the Suffolk landscape of her childhood and snatched every opportunity to return there with her bin-oculars (and ideally with Mamaine) to prowl through the reedbeds and water meadows in search of birds, or wander the sandy lanes, their ragged hedgerows flecked with old man's beard and wild honeysuckle. Failing that, she would repair whenever she could to Dick Wyndham's bolt hole at Tickerage, or trek out to join Mamaine and Arthur in Snowdonia.

Orwell and Celia shared, too, mutual friends in the lively circle of writers, critics and thinkers who revolved around the influential *Horizon* and the just-launched *Polemic*, both journals focused on interrogating the new post-war order and prospects for the unfolding peace. Both were aligned politically to the Left, united in their condemnation of the coruscating lies emanating from the Soviet Union, and equally alarmed by the way that the communists seemed to be gaining bitter ground on the other side of the Channel.

Additionally, Celia's first cousin was the witty and fascinating Inez Holden, one of Orwell's closest friends and, briefly, his lover. I want to take a brief digression into Inez's life because she was one of the most original figures of that era, and after Mamaine's death became increasingly close to Celia and an integral part of our lives as a family. In the mid-1940s, Inez was embroiled in a long on-and-off affair with Humphrey Slater, Celia's editor at *Polemic,* which brought the cousins into regular contact and laid the foundations for their lifelong friendship.

Born, like the twins, into the landed gentry – their mothers Beatrice and Georgina Paget were sisters – at fifteen Inez had left home bound for Paris, putting as much distance as possible between herself and her warring family. Her parents were immensely wealthy, and Inez was brought up in Warwickshire, into the world of the hunt: her flame-haired mother Beatrice was an acknowledged Edwardian beauty and considered the second-best horsewoman in England, keeping fifteen chargers in her stables. Heartless and self-absorbed, her parents not only seemed to loathe one another, they showed their daughter scant love and attention, refusing to pay her school fees. Inez's first memory was of her father shooting at – and missing – her mother during one of their interminable rows.

Beatrice's brother, Uncle Jack (of Ibstock Place), had to step into the breach to pay for Inez's education at a school for poor tradespeople (though, stingy to the last, he would later attempt to reclaim the fees from Inez, with interest),

Inez Holden: 'a torrential talker, an accomplished
mimic', as described by Anthony Powell

'The Impersonation Party', July 1927, featuring the leading lights of
high bohemia. Seated, middle row from left, are Stephen Tennant
dressed as Queen Marie of Roumania, Georgia Sitwell in a false
nose, Inez in a Breton top, and Harold Acton; front row, Talullah
Bankhead as Jean Borotra. Cecil Beaton camps it up, top right.

and when Inez took flight for Paris she unsurprisingly sev-
ered all family ties. Thereafter she lived entirely on her wits
and a fierce defiance. We have no record of how she survived at such a young age in Paris – though she was bright
and beautiful enough to do so, at times clad solely in a borrowed fur coat, or so the story went – nor of exactly when
she returned to giddy post-war London, where, during the
1920s, she started to make her mark as a writer.

A friend of Evelyn Waugh and Anthony Powell, she
was at the epicentre of the set known as the Bright Young

People, and in a well-known photograph from 1927 of Cecil Beaton, Georgia Sitwell, Stephen Tennant, Harold Acton and Talullah Bankhead larking around in fancy dress, Inez stares out of the centre of the group, clear-eyed and arresting in her simple Breton top. Her first three novels were satirical takes on that febrile and feckless *galère*, notably *Sweet Charlatan*, published by Duckworth in 1929.

She was always mysterious about her love life, but certainly counted on a string of admirers. Among these was Augustus John, who made two beautiful chalk drawings of her, portraying the fragile, almost consumptive beauty that led to the nickname of 'Gallopers' among her coterie. Stevie Smith was a close friend, considering her 'vigorous' and 'buccaneering' with 'admirable courage and admirable high heart'. Smith based the sprightly Topaz in *Novel on Yellow Paper* (1936) on Inez and later transformed her into Lopez in her 1949 novel *The Holiday*. Such was the fascination of Inez's personality that she was also immortalised by Anthony Powell, who remembered her as 'a torrential talker, an accomplished mimic' whose conversation was of a 'high and fantastical category', and who may have inspired the adventuress Roberta Payne in his fifth novel *What's Become of Waring?* (1939).

But it was Orwell and H. G. Wells who had the greater influence on Inez. It was inevitable that Orwell and Inez would become close after meeting in April 1940 at a dinner given by Wells; they became better acquainted through their freelance work writing scripts for the BBC in 1941. Both were keenly observant of the world around them; both were left-wing and acted on their political convictions, immersing themselves in working-class life and

culture in Paris and Wigan (Orwell) and in various ord-
nance and aircraft factories during the war (Inez). Both
wrote about their experiences in *Horizon* and elsewhere,
drawing public attention to conditions for the working
poor – for they shared a background of privilege, yet had
chosen to turn their backs on it.

Orwell and Inez swam in the same intellectual and
cultural waters, and a close bond developed between them;
indeed, they briefly became lovers in May 1941, after
Orwell 'pounced' on Inez one afternoon after they'd had
lunch. 'I was surprised by this, by its intensity and urgency,'
she wrote in her diary. However, it did not last: Inez was
about to fall for Humphrey Slater, and was extremely fond
of Orwell's wife Eileen, so a serious affair with George
was never on the cards. George and Inez remained constantly in touch, however, meeting almost weekly, sharing
writing projects and ideas. The Orwells stayed in Inez's
flat at 106 George Street when they were bombed out of
their digs in Mortimer Street in June 1944; they had just
brought their newly adopted baby Richard home from the
hospital and were attempting to forge a new life around
him when the German doodlebug fell, burying all that
they had in dust and debris. Most notably, it was to Inez
that Orwell went first when he heard the news of Eileen's
death in late March 1945.

Inez, then, was among the many links between Celia and
George that gave him hopes for a shared future. In addition, there was a strong physical attraction on Orwell's
part. He had proposed over lunches a couple of times

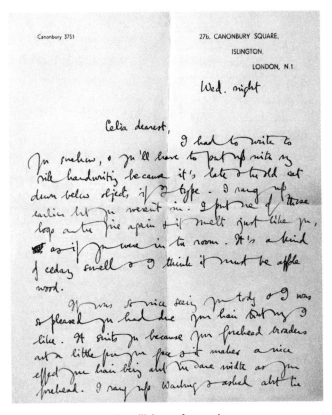

Canonbury 3751

27b, CANONBURY SQUARE,
ISLINGTON,
LONDON, N.1.

Wed. night

Celia dearest,

Orwell's letter of proposal

during January, to no avail, then in a four-page handwritten letter postmarked 31 January, George put his case once more:

> I had to write to you somehow, & you'll have to put up with my vile handwriting because it's late and the old cat down below objects if I type. I rang up earlier but you weren't in. I put one of these logs on the fire again and it smelt just like you, as if you

were in the room. It's a kind of cedary smell & I think it must be applewood.

It was so nice seeing you today & I was so pleased you had done your hair that way I like. […] What I really wanted to tell you is that I love you, which you know already. It's all very reprehensible & undesirable but I can't help it. As I told you I started to love you when you were nice about Richard & I began to want you physically when I saw you walking upstairs in front of me. […] But what I am leading up to, dearest, is to say again that in all this you must think about yourself. If you want to marry me or sleep with me, do, if you don't, don't, but think of it from your own angle because you are young & can make something of your life. You mustn't think about whether you are hurting me, because whatever you do you won't hurt me much. It's not easy to express what I feel towards you. Of course I want you physically, but I feel a deep tenderness towards you, almost like I feel towards Richard. I want you to be happy. You could do me a lot of good if you would be my mistress even for a week, but if you just say you won't or that you have found somebody of your own age who suits you, in a sense I shan't care. In any case it does me good just seeing you.

I'm so looking forward to Tuesday. Don't write to say you can't come, or something. I'm still more looking forward to the following Tuesday so that I can see you with Richard. He'll probably be good for the first quarter of an hour while he's sizing you up & then start trying it on. But if you're tough with him from the start he'll probably decide to knuckle under.

Goodnight my dearest love. I hope you've been able to read this vilely-written letter – I wish I was with you wherever you are.

As Celia later recalled, in the World Service interview,

When I got this letter, I didn't know quite what to do, because I didn't want to marry George, and I didn't want to have an affair with him either, not because I didn't think George was attractive, but because he was such a serious person that you couldn't have an affair with him without getting involved with him, and if you were going to get involved with him, you might as well marry him, and I didn't want to marry him! So I was in a real dilemma about the whole thing. Arthur [Koestler] practically went down on his knees and implored me to marry George, because he simply loved George, and he would have loved to have had George as a brother-in-law. He thought that was a wonderful idea. Anyway, I wrote back to George some rather ambiguous letter, and George said even so, he'd like to go on being friends with me, so we went on seeing each other.

Arthur recognised George's qualities simply years before anybody else did. I mean, at the PEN Club meeting in about 1942 he said in ten years' time he'd bet that George would be a most famous English writer, and the bet was twelve bottles of burgundy. Arthur was so clever himself that he spotted how clever and original George was. And of course they both had the same enlightened view of the Soviet Union, which George had never been taken in about, and he was one of the few Socialist intellectuals who never had. So that was another bond between them. Arthur once said, usually if you meet a writer you've always admired it's a great disillusionment because they're different from their books. But there's one person that didn't apply to. It didn't apply to George Orwell, because he was exactly like his books. Which is true, I think.

Arthur also tried to persuade me to get George to wear a dinner jacket, and what he called 'pep him up a bit'. Which is a terribly funny idea because you couldn't possibly imagine George wearing a dinner jacket. Arthur was rather a hedonist himself, which George rather disapproved of because George wasn't at all like that. He even wrote in an essay about Arthur that he rather disapproved of Arthur's hedonism. But Arthur thought George should be pepped up and not live on strong tea and sardines and shaggy suits. He should go out, not to night clubs, but to rather snappy restaurants. Which didn't really fit George's style of life at all.

George had so whole-heartedly embraced his Orwell persona and its working-class ethos that he genuinely preferred high tea to dinner, and sardines and strong tea to oysters and champagne. He took a dim view of the dives like the Café Royal and the Gargoyle that Celia and her circle frequented – and she recognised that he was far too set in his ways to change.

Naturally Celia confided in Mamaine about the George dilemma; they confided in one another about every matter of the heart. 'I feel sort of trapped,' she wrote. 'If only I could stave it off until the summer, and then G. would go away for six months to Jura, then I might be saved.' Celia did indeed manage to 'stave off' any affair with him, and they continued as friends, as the trail of their letters over the ensuing years shows. Indeed, she continued to help George with Richard, reporting to Mamaine that she had held the fort while George lunched with Bertrand Russell: '[Richard] at once started bawling when he discovered that George wasn't there, and I was afraid that he might go on bawling for three solid hours, which as you know he is quite capable of doing. However I let him wander into every room to make sure that G. really wasn't there [...] and he settled down and was as good as anything . . .'

George had been introduced to the Island of Jura off the west coast of Scotland by David Astor, who arranged a holiday there

MISS CELIA PAGET *at Ciro's.*

for him in September 1945, and he recognised it as a possible solution to his weariness. 'I feel desperately tired and jaded,' he wrote to Arthur Koestler in late March, and again in April 1946: 'I am going away for the whole summer and cutting loose from all this. Everyone keeps coming at me wanting me to lecture, to write commissioned booklets, to join this and that etc. – you don't know how I pine to get free of it all again and have time to think again.' He liked the idea of the island's remoteness and of the simple life of work and husbandry that he could make there. Also he wanted Richard, now an active little boy of two, to have space to run around, without the dangers of London traffic. He was concerned about Richard getting TB, and wanted him to have a country life, as healthy a life as possible.

He used his earnings from *Animal Farm* to buy Barnhill, an isolated and previously uninhabited farmhouse in the east of the island, and in May he set off there, spending his last summer of relative health and strength preparing the house for Richard's arrival with his nanny Susan, putting up shelves, and planting the garden. He continued writing Celia affectionate and chatty letters from the island. In late May he reported, 'It's been incredible weather, so much so that the stream which supplies my cistern has dried up so I can't have a bath until it rains.'

In another letter he described an extraordinary journey he took to the mainland to meet Susan's child off the train at Glasgow:

[…] I set out the day before yesterday morning, but punctured my motor bike on the way and thus missed the boat. I then got a lift first in a lorry, then in a car, and crossed the ferry to the next island in hopes there would be a plane to Glasgow, however the plane was full up, so I took a bus on to Port Ellen, where there would be a boat on Friday morning. Port Ellen was full to the brim owing to a cattle show, all the hotels were full up, so I slept in a cell in the police station along with a lot of other people including a couple with a perambulator. In the morning I got the boat, picked the child up and brought her back, then we hired a car for the first 20 miles and walked the last five home. This morning I got a lift in a motor boat to where my bike was, mended the puncture and rode home – all this in 3 days. […] We go fishing nearly every night, as we are partly dependent on fish for food, and we have also got two lobster pots and catch a certain number of lobsters and crabs. I have now learned to tie up a lobster's claws, which you have to do if you are going to keep them alive, but it is very dangerous, especially when you have to do it in the dark. We also have to shoot rabbits when the larder gets low and grow vegetables. […] With all this you can imagine that I don't do much work – however I have actually begun my new book [which was to be *Nineteen Eighty-Four*] and hope to have four or five chapters done by the time I come back in October. […] I think you would like this place. Do come any time if you want to. […]

In a postscript he asks, tongue in cheek, 'You might ask Freddie [Ayer] from me, now that he has a chair in Mental Philosophy, who has the chair in non-mental philosophy.'

Celia was never to visit George on Jura, partly because her own health continued to be precarious and he had not made any bones about how spartan his life on the island was; and partly because, as his postscript implies, by this time she had fallen in love with Freddie Ayer, and he with her. To her infinite relief, George took the news very well. 'He was wonderful about it,' she told Mamaine,

> said he was very fond of Freddie [...] and suggested we might all three have dinner together one day. I was enormously relieved that he seemed to understand the position at once and that he was so nice about it. He gave me an onyx brooch which he had just bought for me. [...] I am glad to say he said he would like to go on seeing a lot of me, so as far as I'm concerned the position is perfect.

CHAPTER 8

HILL LIFE

In rural Snowdonia, meanwhile, after George and Celia's departure, Arthur and Mamaine's celebrations for New Year 1946 did not go quite as planned. 'We wanted to go to the Oakley for dinner with [Misi] Polanyi,' she wrote to Celia,[16]

> but Arthur got stuck with the car in the garage, it got somehow stuck against the wall and we simply couldn't get it out. So after trying for an hour or more we went back into the house, and tried to make up our minds what to do, as by that time we felt the Oakley to be the most desirable place on the Earth, and felt we couldn't bear to miss the *Sylvester Abend* [New Year] celebrations. We had just eaten the cold duck's carcass and decided to go there by bus and hope for a lift back when K. suggested that we should go to bed in the sitting-room where there was a blazing fire, and he would make bacon and eggs. So we sighed with relief and did that. What did you do?

Round the fireplace

They made up for it soon afterwards with what Mamaine described as

> an awful spell of highbrow social life with Polanyi, the Crawshays and [Bertrand] Russell.[17] [...] Misi Polanyi dined with us and we with him, and he and K had endless conversations about the weight of various particles, the mismic field, the impossibility or not of forming any extrapolation which wd. predict the movements of electrons or God knows what. What with this, a dash of semantics, more physics and emergent vitalism with Russell etc, a discussion with the latter on politics came as a great relief to my weary brain. But my inferiority complex about my ignorance and general dumbness is worse than ever.

The relentless cold and damp of the Welsh winter, compounded by fog, was pretty debilitating for someone with chronic asthma, and Mamaine managed to escape to London in January to see Celia. As she told Edmund Wilson, 'My twinnie relationship is such that I can't go for long without talking to her – indeed I wonder what on earth I would do if K. and I went to live in the States as we talk of doing.' There was no telephone at the farmhouse, so communication was confined to letters or, *in extremis*, telegrams, and Mamaine often found herself too busy to write, even to Celia. She also went to stay (on her own) with Dick Wyndham for a couple of days at Tickerage, the first time she had seen him since their parting. It was not an easy visit: Dick and Arthur were at loggerheads about Palestine, and cordially loathed each other in their mutual jealousy over Mamaine. She found the whole visit very sad, as she admitted to Wilson. Not nearly as sad, however, as Dick must have found it, for he was desperate at having finally lost her.

Mamaine travelled on, via Paris, to Switzerland, where her health picked up in the mountain air, and spent another week in Paris on the way home, where she met Albert and Francine Camus for the first time. She had found Paris very gloomy in its post-war trauma. 'One only has to ask someone the way for them to start in about *les souffrances de la France*,' she wrote to Wilson from Zurich.

> Switzerland, on the other hand, is paradise. I don't
> know whether you can imagine what it is like to
> come from England to a country where everything
> is just as it was before the war. In fact, it looks to

me 100 times better [...]. This morning I put on my new beaver coat and Saks Fifth Ave. sandals and, feeling very elegant though it was of course wasted on the Swiss who have plenty of nice shoes and coats and don't know elegance when they see it anyway, I tripped out to take a look at the shops.

The lashings of food, all the more delicious after British rationing, the crisp air, the snow and the skiing (though she maintained she was bad at it) all filled her with wild excitement. The only drawback was the typewriter she had borrowed: 'it belongs to the hotel and you have to keep putting coins in the slot [...] Also, please forgive my ecstatic ravings: I really am so happy I must rave to somebody.'

She teased Arthur back in food-rationed Wales by sending detailed accounts of what she ate. At the Hotel Peter in Zurich, she recorded:

I am blissfully happy. My meals today were:

6 a.m. an apple & some bread & red wine given me by jovial Germans on the train

10.30 *café complet* at Basle buffet a la Gare (croissant of brown bread)

1.45 *steak garnie* with a terrific Gemisse-platte & *mache* salad, chestnuts & cream

8. mixed grill & half a litre of wine, some of which I left as I simply can't cope with so much food. I believe I could have had goose's liver but it costs a lot & would break my heart: still I may have some tomorrow. LOVE from me xx

Making her way via Gstaad to Wengen, she couldn't contain her excitement:

> I am blissfully happy & feeling terrifically well & I am also very brown, but I suppose I shall lose that on the way back, in Paris. If only my money would last out I would like to stay in Switzerland for another month or so, though I already miss you so much that I might not be able to hold out so long without you. I am so glad I came: I do feel I am now finally cured of the awful effects of last summer. Also my asthma is quite gone, I can climb terrific hills, & constantly do so, without any difficulty . . .

And in Bern, 'where I had such a gay time it nearly killed me', she stayed at the Bellevue – 'the hotel is wonderful, my bath would hold 3 people; I'm afraid it must be awfully expensive.' She quickly found herself whisked up into a social whirl:

> On Saturday night I went to a big dinner party, followed by a ball at something called (modestly enough) le Cercle de Grande Societé. I wonder how I was ever let in to this august and lofty institution; but I was, and spent the evening dancing with various ministers & with an incredibly pompous gent called le chef du Protocol, whose chief job in life seems to be to decide who goes through doors first, & who got so into the habit of introducing diplomats to me that he started introducing me as Mme P. de la Legation de Grande Bretagne! Then I sat up at the bar till 3

with Tony Bower – the night before I was up till 3.30, the night before that till 2.30, so I don't know how much longer I can hold out.

Tony Bower was an amusing, clever American contemporary of Connolly's and Ayer's from their Oxford days, 'a gossip columnist without a column', in Maurice Bowra's words. He crops up often in Mamaine's diaries and seemed to be in regular attendance. Being gay, he posed no emotional complications and their friendship was based upon gossip, good humour and a zest for life, which he had in abundance.

On she went to Geneva, where she was introduced to Tristan Tzara, a Romanian–French avant-garde poet and former ringleader of the Dada movement. Impresario, performer, sometime surrealist, cultural gadfly, he had fought for the Republicans in the Spanish Civil War and later joined the French Resistance. By now a somewhat superannuated *enfant terrible* (he was born in 1896), over a very long lunch he tried and failed to persuade Mamaine to accompany him to Vienna for a week. 'He is a Stalinist of the deepest dye, and really, all his ideas are completely mad. He is bringing out <u>8</u> books, mostly, I gather, *éditions de luxe* of various poems (including one about me, he says!). I don't much like what I have read, and can't quite see the point of doing that sort of thing at this stage.'

Returning in March to Wales, she admitted to Celia, 'My God it was cold when we arrived back here; I put on twice as many clothes as I ever wore in Switzerland, and yet I shivered for two days. Now thank God it is warmer. But I must say coming back here makes one realise what

Mamaine with Nellie

an austere life K. and I lead.' She consoled herself with the beauty of the countryside, with 'curlews whistling away [...] I have discovered a wonderful beach not far from here where there are all sorts of waders to be seen at low tide, when you come up we must go into this. I have twice seen buzzards near here, the other day I saw about six.' The twins' mutual love of birds and birdsong could usually be relied upon to raise their spirits.

Now that Mamaine was back in Arthur's orbit, her natural high spirits were tempered, and her quality of life was entirely dictated by his moods which swung alarmingly between extremes of depression and elation, depending on how his work was going. Mamaine had to run the household, entertain their frequent guests, work flat out on editing and typing up Arthur's current book-in-progress and correspondence, and somehow find time for her own reading, painting and piano playing. In June 1946, Arthur's former girlfriend Daphne and her husband Henri Henrion were staying for a few days: 'Daphne is very nice indeed and I get on very well with her,' Mamaine wrote to Celia. 'But K. has been in an absolutely fiendish temper, so life has hardly been worth living. However, this is only because he is doing hellish work, correcting endless French versions of his books and play, and therefore can't get on with his book; by Thursday he should have finished and then his temper will improve – I hope; otherwise I shall soon retire to a mental home.' She too had piles of correspondence to deal with – 'yesterday there were 21 letters and today lots more. It is a stinking bore. It makes us both frightfully bad-tempered.' They tried taking on a daily help from the village, but she was 'paralysed in one arm and hardly speaks any English! Mrs. T takes all morning to wash up three plates, and the whole thing is very unsatisfactory.' Nevertheless they gritted their teeth and kept Mrs T on, to give Mamaine an occasional break from domestic chores.

When there were no guests Mamaine managed to find the time to do some painting – entirely untutored, almost primitive landscapes scenes in oil. 'I have done an awfully nice little picture, which I am terrifically pleased with. It is of the house and mountains (more or less). God it is pretty (I think).' Her landscapes are richly suffused with colour, immediate, raw – her few surviving canvases, full of naive charm, now hang in my own cottage.

But with the relentless demands of Arthur's work, how was she to find her own fulfilment? This was Mamaine's constant dilemma. She was reading widely and studying psychology herself, filling several small books with notes on her reading; she also longed to paint more, listen to music on the Third Programme, and have time for her

Breakfast at Bwlch Ocyn

own thoughts and correspondence with Celia and friends like Edmund Wilson. It was a constant source of friction between her and Arthur, and they revisited the subject again and again, to no avail. Arthur needed to dictate his books and to palm off on her all his other worries in order to concentrate fully on his writing, but, as she confided to Celia, 'It is not a question that I am bad at it, for I am by now fairly efficient, but it is true that I loathe it and apparently my face when K is dictating to me is so filled with loathing, boredom and despair that he simply can't bring himself to do it.'

Arthur had the grace to admit that he was being demanding, as she related to Celia. "'I know I am offering you very little [he conceded] and asking the impossible, namely, that you should be attractive and a good hostess and a good cook and at the same time a good and full-time secretary and collaborator." "Well, I said, I guess you are. All I can say is, that I will try and adapt myself . . . but I don't altogether like the idea, and what's more I'm afraid that if I do as you suggest you will get to think of me only as a secretary in the end." To which he agreed.' She could see no way out: 'it's heads you win tails I lose for me,' as she put it. However, cheerfulness reasserted itself in the same letter: 'There is one consoling aspect of my life, which is that K's predictions of everything are always on the gloomy side, and are generally wrong . . . whereas I generally succeed in the end in making things work out the way I want, by dint of dogged perseverance.'

Though she railed at 'sitting for hours while K slowly and laboriously utters his truths about higher psychology at the rate of four words a minute', dogged perseverance along with her capitulation to Arthur's wishes usually got them through. 'It is K's fervent desire that I should collaborate in his work and make it the centre of my life as it is of his, and that is why, for instance, he gets impatient if I bother about lunch, since he rightly thinks that this means I'm not concentrating enough on his books.' However, she tried to be philosophical to Celia: 'If one really wants to live with somebody difficult like K it is no good if one is always thinking about one's own interests. [. . .] I will only say that the reason I think this worth doing, is that I think K is a very worthwhile person; otherwise of course it would be a waste of time.'

This sentiment was not shared by Ging-Ging and Jacko who were, after all, among the twins' closest relatives, even if some distance apart in choice of lifestyle. Arthur, a deracinated intellectual of dubious origins and even more dubious convictions, was, in their eyes, even less suitable husband-material for Mamaine than Dick

Wyndham had been; in fact, they couldn't imagine anyone with fewer qualifications for the role, which caused
some pain to Mamaine, who was still deeply devoted to
her aunt. Ging-Ging, who we can be certain had never
got anywhere near to reading one of Arthur's books, took
to referring to him sniffily as '*un écrivain de trente-sixième
ordre*'* prompting Mamaine to write to Celia, 'I'm sorry
Auntie is so inconsolable about me. What can one do? Do
drum it into the fam. what a nice chap K is and how happy
we are, anyway.'

However arduous the days of toiling over typescripts
and correspondence, they were enlivened by entertaining, sometimes riotous evenings with various friends and
neighbours – Bertrand Russell and his abrasive wife Peter;
Richard Hughes, author of *High Wind in Jamaica*; Mark
and Irene Sontag, refugees from Austria who became
close friends – at all of which, inevitably, Arthur drank
too much, with often comic results. 'Lovely evening with
the Hughes at their house last night,' Mamaine scribbled to
Celia. 'Arthur got rather tight and on the way back along
the sand (they live on the estuary opposite Port M[eirion])
he kept falling down; once he walked off a wall where
he thought there were some steps and there weren't; then
he disappeared into a hole, and shortly afterwards was
seen almost up to his waist in the sea! It was all great
fun. Love from Twin.' During dinner with the Sontags,
'K tried to make some Austrian *knödels* with jam in the
middle but they swelled for some reason to the size of foot-
balls and the jam quite disappeared and they tasted like
canon-balls – *Kanonknodel* as Sontag said. This gave us all

---

* 'a thirty-sixth-rate writer'

hysterics.' So it was not all highbrow conversation, to Mamaine's profound relief. Nevertheless she did ask Edmund Wilson, some-what plaintively, 'Tell me, do people in America talk all the time about seman-tics and logical positivism? In Wales they seem to, and I must say it's a bit much.'

Arthur with Joe and Dinah

Relations with Bertrand and Peter Russell were always volatile. In May, according to Mamaine, 'Peter Russell seems to have completely bitched up (a) our relations with Russell and (b) Arthur's world-saving scheme, in which at first Russell expressed great willingness to cooperate.' In August the Russells broke the stalemate by asking Arthur and Mamaine to dinner, an invitation that Mamaine accepted with alacrity. 'If it had been Arthur he would probably have said yes on condition that you take back everything you have ever said or something, but needless to say I didn't take a firm line of any kind, rightly or wrongly, but just said yes, so now we're all palsy-walsies again.' Russell spent most of the evening talking to Mamaine:

Arthur said this was because he (Russell) has a crush on me . . . I said you have an *idée fixe* that every man not demonstrably homosexual has a crush on me, and Arthur said well it is so. Then he made a little speech about how when he looked at all the other women he knew (giving examples of some exceptionally frightful ones) he couldn't help thinking that he had got a winner.

She added that Peter Russell never let Bertrand get a word in edgeways if she could help it, and, 'Today she said in front of him that he couldn't at the outside live for more than another 20 years – we all nearly died of embarrassment.'

Even with these respites, Mamaine increasingly felt the strain of Arthur's wild mood swings, which were often exacerbated by alcohol and were exhausting for both of them. Mamaine did her level best to cheer him during his spells of profound gloom and to offset his intrinsic pessimism. But she confided in Celia that she found the situation increasingly worrying: 'He says he is so much more of a manic-depressive – mostly depressive – than he used to be. But he still says I am his only prop, and though I have not been much good in that direction lately I intend to go on trying.' And a few months later: 'I am afraid he is starting a period of very bad temper, but perhaps it will blow over. I just try to shut my eyes and ears and withdraw into my shell. I feel pretty dismal and there is no news . . .' And again: 'I am terribly depressed, chiefly because life with K seems to get more and more difficult. Lately he seems to have been nagging more than usual; perhaps not; perhaps I am less able to react well than formerly.'

In between these bouts of gloom, however, he would surprise Mamaine, or 'Mermaid' as he still called her, with his high spirits and good humour. Celia was amused to hear that,

K is turning poet in his middle age [he was 41]. He now wakes me every day with a song, the words of which are as follows (composed by him):

'Rise and shine / Sweetheart mine / For the clock is striking / Half past nine.'

As it is usually half past eight, these words are generally omitted and only the tune (very out of tune at that) is sung.

Indeed, Mamaine had turned poet too, celebrating the anniversary of their arrival at Bwlch Ocyn in late August with the following doggerel:

POEM FOR AN ANNIVERSARY
Bwlch Ocyn, Manod, Blaenau Ffest-
iniog, Merionethshire – you've guessed:
'Tis the abode of ARTHUR K.
One year ago this very day
K, who from sunnier climes had come
To make in CAMBRIA his home,
Arrived with MERMAID to begin
With her a life of carefree sin.
The antique house a little room contained
New-built when K his needs to JIM explained;
Here K did work; and, seeking not prosperity
Nor fame, penned volumes destined for posterity.
Also, as he sat writing at his desk,
Hastening to complete th'appointed task,
He found that here a slate, there a loose pane
Left him exposed to the wind and rain.
But soon JOHN OWEN JONES and MR LLOYD

From dawn to dusk were steadily employed
Mending a broken window, door or slate
To give protection from the Welsh climate.
Often at evening, with his two trusty Hounds
JOSEPH and DINA, K would tour the grounds
And from some pinnacle or knoll inspect
Th'autumnal hills with crimson fern bedeck'd.
Or, if in sorrowful mood, he'd take the car
All cares to banish in PORTMEIRION's bar,
Where he would find HENRY, TEDDY and JIM
Eager to drink and talk and jest with him.
Apricot brandy, orange curacao,
Gin, rum and whisky did freely flow;
The Sage LORD RUSSELL would with K rehearse all
The arguments against the Universal,
Or, while they watched young CONRAD's lively antics,
RUPERT and K would talk about Semantics.
And when, the evening over, he did wing
His homeward way, K to himself would sing:
    Biology, neurology
    Aesthetics and psychology
    Ethics, epistemology
    The art of terminology
I'll study, and with them do I resolve
The riddle of the Universe I'll solve.
As time went by, attracted by its fame,
Many a pilgrim to Bwlch Ocyn came.
ROTHSCHILD and CROSSMAN, ORWELL,
CELIA, FREDDIE,
BRENDA and WANDA, DOMINIQUE and
TEDDY.

Many a cheerful evening thus was spent
In eating, drinking, music, argument,
With DICK and ZITA, EMILY their poodle
MARK and IRENE (and th'atomic Knoedle).
So from now on each year will ARTHUR K
And MERMAID drink together on this day;
Where'er they be, they will this happy date
With wine and song together celebrate.

This they did – though I can't vouch for the song – but after their celebratory dinner Arthur became more depressed and worried than ever about the effect his multifarious neuroses would have on Mamaine's happiness, saying that for her sake she should leave him, which she refused to do. Four more days of gloom later, he made an almighty scene and stormed out of a dinner with friends at Portmeirion, reiterating remorsefully the following day that Mamaine must leave him if she hoped to retain any of her friends. Again, she managed to console him. 'But there's no getting away from the fact,' she told Celia, 'that writers in general, and K in particular, are not made for domestic happiness – they *need* loneliness and unhappiness and dread peace and security. Still, K said that our year here has been one of the best & happiest of his life, & I suppose the same applies to me.' There were also money worries, and Arthur's ruse to counter them was to have one 'austerity week' every fourth week, buying nothing but tins of corned beef and sardines. On his departure for London, however, Arthur showed great concern about Mamaine getting depressed in his absence and tried to persuade her to come too;

failing in that, he ordained that she must drink half a bottle of wine every evening without fail. Alcohol was always his panacea, but one that, for him, created more problems than it solved.

CHAPTER 9

RAPTURE

By autumn 1946, both Mamaine and Arthur felt in need of a break, and Koestler's one and only play, *Twilight Bar,* an exercise in science fiction about a failed utopia, was about to be staged in Paris. Arthur was granted a visa and at the start of October set off to spend a few weeks there overseeing rehearsals, with Mamaine to follow soon after. This was his first visit since the end of the war, and since a French edition of *Darkness at Noon* (translated as *Le Zéro et l'Infini,* or *Zero and Infinity*) had been published in 1945. It had been an overnight sensation, selling 300,000 copies by the time he arrived in October 1946, and an astonishing half a million copies within two years. This was not just thanks to the French Communist party buying it up in bulk to stop it getting into the hands of citizens, as was rumoured; those very citizens queued in droves outside the offices of his publishers, Calmann-Lévy, whenever new editions went to press, and secondhand copies changed hands for many times their original price. Koestler was now a prime literary lion in France and feted as such.

He had an ulterior motive in visiting Paris: he hoped to use his newfound celebrity to persuade the politicians and intellectuals of the Left Bank that communism had succeeded fascism as the greatest threat to Europe. He was exasperated by what he saw as the gullibility of the younger generation in falling for the lures of the Soviet system and was determined to re-emphasise its horrors and its insidious reach.

The bestselling French edition of *Darkness at Noon*

Twilight Bar had already been a terrible flop in New York and he expected the worst in Paris; it is hardly surprising that he never wrote another play. But he wasted no time in introducing himself to the circle of existentialist writers whom he admired, Albert Camus foremost among them. Camus, in trench coat with eternal cigarette, was as well known as editor of the former Resistance journal *Combat* as he was as author of *L'Étranger* and *Le Mythe de Sisyphe.** As a crusading journalist in Algeria and France, an actor and director and contributor to numerous journals, he had known several years of triumph, of success crowning success. At *Combat,* Camus was promoting the idea of a Third Way in politics, deploring both Stalinist dictatorship and American capitalism in favour of a middle path that he elaborated upon in a series of articles titled *Ni victimes ni bourreaux.*† Camus was immediately sympathetic to Koestler's anti-communist agenda, promising to give him support, and their friendship was instantaneous.

---

* *The Stranger* and *The Myth of Sisyphus*

† 'Neither Victims nor Executioners'

Not only did their political principles coincide, but they affected a similar style and shared similar tastes, as Arthur put it, 'in wining, dining and running after women'.

Soon after meeting Camus, Arthur doorstepped his neighbours Jean-Paul Sartre and Simone de Beauvoir. Their admiration of one another's work was mutual, despite Koestler's challenging opening gambit to Sartre: 'You are a better novelist than I am, but not such a good philosopher,' followed by a discourse on his recent thinking that led Simone de Beauvoir to conclude that Koestler was certainly a less good philosopher than he was a novelist. Initially she found him vain and self-important, 'But he was also full of warmth, life and curiosity,' she wrote in her memoirs,

> the passion with which he argued was unflagging; he was always ready, at any hour of the day or night, to talk about any subject under the sun. He was generous with his time, with himself, and also with his money; he had no taste for ostentation, but when one went out with him he always wanted to pay for everything and never counted the cost.

Mamaine she described as 'very pretty, with a sharp wit; graceful and fragile, she was already suffering from the lung infection to which she succumbed some ten years later.'[18]

En route to Paris Mamaine had stayed in London, catching up with Celia and various friends, and she joined Arthur in Paris in late October, only to discover that he had been having a fling with the wife of a Russian journalist – which plunged her into a black depression.

She acknowledged that it was nothing serious, but it was humiliating to see him flirt with the 'blonde bombshell' and quite destroyed her equilibrium and *joie de vivre*. She also found Arthur drinking heavily and full of self-doubt, convinced that *Twilight Bar* would fail in Paris as it had in New York. The play opened on 23 October as *Bar du cré-puscule* and, as predicted, was slated by the critics and pronounced a 'disaster' by Sartre; even Mamaine was forced to admit after the first night that it was a 'God-awful flop'.

Despite this setback they were quickly drawn into a frenetic whirl of drinks, dinners and parties with the Left Bank set – principally Sartre and de Beauvoir, André Malraux, and Albert and Francine Camus. 'On Sunday we started the day at 10.30 a.m. with Sartre and Simone de Beauvoir, [Harold] Kaplan (of *Partisan Review*), Teddy Kolleck and his wife, Sylvester and Pauline [Gates] and Arthur's friend Leo – a not very successful *salade russe*,' begins a typical letter. The writer André Malraux and his wife Madeleine were frequent dining companions; Malraux had been a prominent communist fellow-traveller in the 1930s (and subsequently a distinguished member of the Resistance) before experiencing a Gaullist epiphany in 1945 and serving in de Gaulle's provisional government as Minister of Information.

'I want to tell you all about our dinner with Malraux last night,' Mamaine wrote to Celia.

> He is very rich and has an enormous and flashy flat in the banlieue at Boulogne s/Seine.[…] It is horrible and very bare and *ungemütlich*.* The dinner started

---

* 'un-cosy'

with oysters, and the Malraux had the bizarre idea of drinking whisky with them, till I said this would very likely cause the immediate death of all, whereupon they suggested gin fizz! […] Malraux is fascinating but not in the least attractive; K, who is rather in love with him, was very astonished and relieved when I told him this. He obviously has an ex-ophthalmic goitre, for his eyes protrude and he talks non-stop to the accompaniment of curious sounds at the back of his nose and throat – a kind of tic. He talks in a kind of telegraphese which is very hard to follow; indeed I couldn't keep up at all some of the time, and K said nobody can, and he (K) has to take time off by not listening to Malraux's anecdotes, otherwise the effort of concentration is too great.

The oysters were followed by chicken soaked in brandy with prunes and slices of lemon, and a delicious chocolate cream. Mamaine was particularly amused by the sight of the two writers together: the normally ebullient Arthur 'unusually humble and hardly able to get in a word edgeways, Malraux obviously very anxious to impress K, show off to me, etc.[…] He gives the impression of being very inhuman and impersonal, and it is difficult to see how anyone ever establishes an intimate contact with him; this is also K's opinion, though he knows Malraux well . . .' Malraux could talk for France, and indeed as Minister of Culture under de Gaulle from 1958–69 he would later be paid to do so, travelling the world as a roving cultural ambassador, baffling his audiences with pyrotechnic speeches punctuated with his nervous verbal tic. On

The Schéhérazade nightclub

home ground, however, he was to make an effective and impressive minister, clearing up historic Paris after the devastation of the war years, and bringing French culture to the provinces.

The brief interlude with the blonde spy (as they called her) was over, but both recognised it as another of Arthur's subconscious ruses to drive Mamaine away – which he now acknowledged were part and parcel of his neurotic masochism, 'and anyway only made because he knows damned well I shall refuse to go, which as you know I always do,' she explained to Celia. They had sat up almost all night discussing it, which in Mamaine's view was understandable – 'one must do something about people who have no twin to discuss these things with'. Celia was always her first choice of confidante and would be the first to hear of the passionate feelings for Camus that were soon to take over Mamaine's entire existence.

It started in the Schéhérazade, a Russian nightclub in the ninth arrondissement, only a few days later. Arthur and Mamaine had quickly become friendly with Sartre and Beauvoir, cemented one evening in Sartre's flat. 'Sartre is simply charming,' Mamaine wrote, 'and while he is talking one feels that existentialism must be the thing, without always having much idea what it is. He and K get on very well, and we both get on like a house on fire with Simone de Beauvoir . . .' A few days later, the four of them met up for dinner at an Arab bistro with Albert and Francine Camus (whom Mamaine thought 'very beautiful and nice'), then on to a little 'dancing' nearby. 'Here for the first time in my life I danced with K, and also saw the engaging spectacle of him lugging the Castor [their nick-name for de Beauvoir, the French for 'beaver'] (who has I think hardly ever danced in her life) round the floor while Sartre (who ditto) lugged Mme Camus.' From there they went on to the Schéhérazade, 'a posh Russian nightclub. Here one is plunged in almost total darkness and a great many violinists wander around playing soulful Russian music into one's ear. At first everyone except K was very much against this place, but after a while they all started to enjoy it no end.' There they drank copious quantities of vodka and champagne, at Arthur's expense. 'It was very difficult to get K away [...] but finally at about 4 we got going and went to a bistro where we ordered *soupe à l'oignon*, oysters, white wine and various other things. By that time Sartre was simply roaring drunk [...]' Arthur suddenly became aggressive and threw a piece of bread at Mamaine, hitting her squarely in the eye, about which he was later very apologetic.

Finally we left (I suppose it was about 7, anyway it was broad daylight) and after that it took me until 8.30 to get K home – we wandered along the river, which looked incredibly beautiful with those lovely lemon-green and yellow poplars with their black trunks, and the houses reflected in the water and the early morning light, and K got very sentimental and wept profusely. Now my eye is completely black and I have to borrow a black patch.[…] We slept all day.

In her diary she relates how on the journey home she stood outside a *pissoire* while Arthur, from within, yelled, 'Don't leave me, I love you, I'll always love you!' into the night sky.

Beauvoir's account of the evening throws more light on Arthur's preoccupations: 'Koestler grew gloomy […] "It's impossible to be friends if you differ about politics!" he said in an accusing tone. He rehashed his old grudges about Stalin's Russia, accusing Sartre and even Camus of trying to compromise with the Soviets. We didn't take his lugubriousness seriously; we were not aware of the passionate depths of his anti-Communism.' It was Camus who brokered a truce by claiming, 'What we have in common, you and I, is that for us individuals come first; we prefer the concrete to the abstract, people to doctrines, we place friendship above politics.' Despite Koestler's objections – 'Impossible! Impossible!' – they concluded, with the flush of alcohol running through their veins, that their happiness in one another's company proved that Camus's claim was indeed true.

There was more weeping and histrionics between Sartre and de Beauvoir as the evening wore on, as she recorded: '[…] when I found myself alone with Sartre in the streets of Paris at dawn I began to sob over the tragedy of the human condition; as we crossed the Seine I leaned on the parapet of the bridge. "I don't see why we don't throw ourselves into the river!" "All right, then, let's throw ourselves in!" said Sartre, who was finding my tears contagious and had shed a few himself. We got home about eight in the morning.' Sartre was scheduled to give a talk that afternoon under the aegis of UNESCO on 'The Writer's Responsibility', which by dint of stuffing himself with orthedrine he managed at least to prepare. 'I thought to myself as I went into the packed amphitheatre: "If they had seen him at six this morning!"' de Beauvoir concluded.[19]

Mamaine revealed to Celia that at the Schéhérazade she and Camus, neither of whom had drunk much, went off to dance at the other end of the dance floor, and that he told her how strongly he had been attracted to her at their first meeting that spring. She was in turn smitten with him, and flippantly told him that Arthur never minded her flirting with men with whom it meant nothing, to which he replied that he refused to be that kind of man – and that she was someone he could fall in love with. 'Twin, you have no idea how attractive and *sympathique* Camus is,' she added, obviously touched by his attention and already prey to powerful emotions.

Following the extravaganza at the Schéhérazade, Arthur and Mamaine met the Camuses for a drink before Arthur caught the train back to London. Mamaine had decided to stay on in France and spend a week in the south-west;

Albert Camus

when she got back to her hotel room she found a bouquet of roses with a note from Camus. She met him for a drink a couple of days later: 'we were rather shy,' she recorded in her diary, '& he said he couldn't forget the other evening at the Schéhérazade.' She told him of her plans to tour the south-west of France with a couple of friends, and they agreed they should probably meet on her return. 'Then Francine arrived & we dined in an empty restaurant in the *quartier*, very gaily.'

The following day, realising that she might be getting out of her depth, she met Camus again to tell him that she had decided not to see him on her return, only to find more roses and another letter awaiting her in her rooms afterwards. A walk together in the Bois de Boulogne the following evening sealed their bond. He wasted no time in telling her that he was in love with her, and knew that if they had an affair, neither of them would be able to treat it lightly. '*Je ne peux pas te quitter . . . je ne suis bien qu'auprès de toi*', he told her, to which she protested that she was not sure she took it all as seriously as he did.* Also that she loved Arthur, that he was her whole life, and that she would probably kill herself if he left her. Yet, that being so, how could she feel as she did about Camus? She added that there was no question of keeping any liaison from Arthur – with which Camus concurred, saying he had been turning this over in his mind himself over the past few days.

He suggested they should go away together, to Provence, but she made no commitment and remained 'harassed by doubts'. Nevertheless, she was powerfully drawn to him, and touched by his protestations of love. 'You would think,' she wrote to Celia,

> that it is easy for me now simply to say, well, it's clear what we have to do, and I'm not going to see you any more. And I more or less did say that. But it is hell doing it because of the intolerable feeling that one's missing a unique chance, of the kind of which there are very few in one's whole life. However I expect that under the stress of emotion I am dramatising and exaggerating the importance of the whole thing wildly.

She added, 'How all this can happen to a girl with a black eye is a mystery to me!'

In the end, Mamaine travelled south to Toulouse alone, meeting up with two friends there for a motoring trip round the south-west. The three visited Pau, St Jean de Luz, Biarritz, crossed over into Spain, and back through

---

* 'I can't give you up . . . I only feel happy when I'm with you.'

the Landes to Bordeaux, sometimes in the wake of the Virgin of Boulogne ('a horrible white virgin in a boat') who was also touring the country in a drift of blue and white streamers and sermons in Basque. Her spirits were high, as she wrote to Arthur from Pau:

> Darling, We came here yesterday from Toulouse [...] The hotels we have been staying in so far are horrible, their squalor & inefficiency is only equalled by their expense: at Toulouse one couldn't get breakfast at all, here one can but it costs 150frs! It is terribly cold, I should think it is freezing, there is no sun, & one can't see the Pyrenees. But I am enjoying myself as I so love going to towns I don't know and the drive here was lovely.

She did not confess to Arthur that there was a letter from Camus waiting for her at the Hôtel Splendide in Bordeaux, suggesting they meet in Avignon the following Monday.

She met Camus off the train in Avignon. The next note Celia received was dated just four days later: 'Just a line to say that I am having a *wonderful* time, more like a fairy tale than real life. It is just perfect from every point of view [...]' It was written from the Hôtel Crillon, where Mamaine and Camus were staying. And a few days after that, on Sunday 24 November: 'C. is writing an article, I have time to write you a short scrawl. It is literally the first time we have been separated (he is in the next room) for more than 5 minutes since he arrived here on Monday night.' She goes on to explain that, despite her happiness, she is not really in love with Camus, 'though he is perfect & I can find no

Camus in Provence, photographed by Mamaine

faults or shortcomings in him at all'. She qualified this with, 'almost perfect – & I say almost because I suppose he must have *some* faults'. But he was certain of his love, and told her he would like to live with her, 'and if I did this we could go and live in Provence, which I've always wanted to do, & I could have children [which Arthur refused to countenance], & I'm sure we would be happy, for a while at any rate [...] It is so incredible and undeserved that he should feel the way he does,' she confided.

From Avignon they set out to explore the Provençal landscape, where Camus had decided he wanted to settle, and her diary records their enchanted time together:

Arles – the cloisters of St Trophime (the sad medieval saints and the lauriers roses), the Alys sunset, the Algerian pedlar in the café who called us both '*tu*' and talked with C about Rabat; wandering through the dark narrow streets in search of a bistro to dine in; the slow train back – walking to Villeneuve (*pour le marché* . . .), lunch in the little hotel . . . C buying me a yellow jumper on the way back, sleeping, him waking me with some red roses (the concierge when C asked him to get them said '*Ah, Monsieur, comme je vous comprends*'), the young man playing Bach in the bar who turned out to have recognised C, & asked us to dine & stay the night at his château at Sommières. Both his parents had been shot by the Germans. [. . .] Dancing tangos in the Spanish nightclub, & the beautiful Spanish woman with her interminable stories about the Spanish war.

Then Lourmarin, the pretty fountain opposite the bar, the walks through the olive groves, & looking for a house for C; the lovely light almond trees, red fruit trees, yellow earth, brown village with blue shutters; & sitting on the hill with C's head in my lap & the sun coming through the trees, looking over towards the hills of Haute Provence. Pastis by the stove in the café; C saying *'Pendant cette semaine tu m'as rendu aussi heureux et aussi malheureux qu'on peut rendre un homme.'**

As Mamaine wrote to Celia of Lourmarin: 'Twin: it is the most beautiful place in the world, I'm sure. C. wants to live there, & so do I with all my heart. The sun shone all the time, and the earth was red & yellow & brown, & imagine red and yellow fruit trees, olive trees, poplars, almond and mulberry trees (pale green) ilexes, cypresses and firs, & god knows what . . . oh, what happiness!' She took a few photographs as they wandered around, and I recently discovered the negatives, never to my knowledge printed up till now – hurried snaps, the essence of informality, but redolent of the region and the late autumn light. Camus would indeed buy a house there, in what has subsequently been named rue Albert Camus. On the edge of the village, with views over the valley to the west, it is an idyllic spot. Despite her earlier intention to tell Arthur of any affair, Mamaine ends her letter by swearing Celia to secrecy: 'I have decided to conceal from K

---

* 'During this week you've made me as happy and as wretched as any man can be.'

everything . . . what we have done together is too great an infidelity for anyone to bear.'

Nevertheless, she and Camus both acknowledged that this brief interlude of happiness and passion was just that: an interlude, a *coup de foudre,* which could not last; they had to return to Paris and to their respective lives and relationships. They could not take their eyes off each other in the train on the way back; they both tried to do so for five minutes, and failed. She told Camus he would forget her, and he replied, Of course, one forgets everything, but that he would simply not want to live in a world in which he had forgotten her. 'So my head is whizzing round,' she wrote to Celia, 'but in the meantime, nothing is changed. However much one may long for real happiness I don't think one can let people down – besides my happiness is really with K, I think this most likely.' She tried to explain to Celia Arthur's attitude towards her, which, she wrote, was one of admiration and trust. 'I don't know why but he has got it into his head that I deserve both, how wrongly you know . . . It is true, as Freddie [Ayer] said, that he doesn't treat me as an equal, he treats me as if I were above him. Oh twinnie it is all too complicated to talk about in a letter.'

Irascible and demanding as Arthur was, Mamaine had, after all, decided to throw in her lot with him; she was committed to him and to the long haul, as she might have put it. But with Camus she had found love on another level: one that freed her to be herself, without let or hindrance. They had enjoyed an interlude out of life, without past or future, without ties or responsibilities to others, a time to be with one another exclusively and to be everything to one another – and that, they both acknowledged, could not last.

It was a love in stark contrast to all the other loves in Mamaine's life: she was drawn to difficult and demanding men, and her relationships were frequently stormy and tormented. They exhausted her physically and emotionally, even if they sustained her on an intellectual level. With Camus there was no friction; instead, a rare collusion of minds and hearts that they both found profoundly liberating. In one of Camus's letters to my mother after Mamaine's death he was to write, 'And with her, I always felt free (you know how it is difficult to be free, even with those one loves the most). I was free and in consequence it was easier for me to be better with her than I was with others.' They found their best selves with one another, put simply. How bitter to leave that discovery behind them and return to their everyday lives, compromised and complicated as they were.

Although the affair left an indelible impression on Camus – and although he had joked to friends, even after the birth of their twins Jean and Catherine in 1945, that he was never cut out for marriage – he was irrevocably bound to Francine, his beautiful, loyal, loving but psychologically fragile wife who hailed from Oran in western Algeria. He was serially unfaithful to her over the years, notably and most publicly with the Spanish actress Maria Casares, but he never seriously contemplated leaving her, and indeed suffered almost telepathically alongside her during her depressions and breakdown – which, of course, were made all the more acute by his infidelities.

Despite their decision to give one another up, Mamaine and Camus met a couple more times back in Paris, once outside Le Dôme where Mamaine arrived half an hour late – having mistaken the time of their rendezvous – to find the café closed and Camus pacing, clearly upset and afraid she had changed her mind. In the event he said, philosophically, 'What does a reasonable man do in such circumstances? He corrects his proofs,' and indeed he had started correcting the proofs of *La Peste* which he had in his pocket. 'How silly of you to think I wasn't coming,' protested Mamaine, and, 'he frowned and said, almost crossly, "*Mais tu ne comprends pas – je t'aime.*"'* After a walk in the Luxembourg Gardens they settled in another café where he talked her through scenes from *La Peste,* and the ideas that lay behind them. But Mamaine could no longer postpone her return to Arthur in Wales, and they braced themselves to part.

Mamaine's diary comes to a halt at this point, but it appears that she decided, after all, to tell Arthur about the affair, now that it was to all intents over. How could she continue to live with him with any integrity while harbouring this huge, overwhelming secret: it was far too significant an emotional event to ignore. She admitted to Camus by letter that she had told Arthur the essentials (sparing him the details) and Camus was appalled and poured out his dismay combined with his love for her in a long letter. Though he addresses her lightly as 'Twinkie *chérie*', his letter is drenched in pain. The days that followed her departure, he wrote, were '*comme les jours morts*' – days of death. The only thing at all alive in him was the hope of

---

* 'But you don't understand – I love you.'

receiving a letter from her. And now it had arrived, it filled him with despair. In speaking to Arthur of their love, she had taken away from him the one thing he still had left: the unsullied memory of their happiness. He had thought that the memory was theirs alone, and she had now forced him to share it with another; reading her letter, he said, made him feel that he was losing her a second time.

He went on to admit that after his initial anguish – during which he could not even think of Avignon without feeling torn apart – he began to think more about Mamaine and less about himself and arrived at some understanding. 'I was aware of nothing but my affection ['*tendresse*'] for you, my wish to help you and to know you are happy, even without me.' One must try to be happy in the life one has chosen, he averred, and the best way for him to help her in this would be to maintain silence, so that is what he had decided to do – but he did not want her to think that his silence was remotely hostile: it was the only way he could find to express his love for her. And, now that their affair had no future, he could at last tell her with utter simplicity that the days he had spent with her were the happiest of his life, and that he would never forget them.

The confession to Arthur had cost Mamaine dear, too. Of all possible rivals for Mamaine's affection, Arthur could hardly have imagined a more alarming one than Camus, an intellectual equal whom he liked and greatly respected, and who he knew was irresistible to women. Arthur's pride, moreover, was wounded; Mamaine had kept at bay all other admirers to date, so this was indeed a bitter blow, and all the more so for the fact that she could not entirely hide from him how much it meant to her, and how she could not stop herself pining for Camus's company. He took the news with reasonable equanimity at the time (he had after all had a brief fling not only with the 'blonde bombshell' but also with Simone de Beauvoir while in Paris, so he could hardly grandstand) but the jealousy Arthur now felt towards Camus was to simmer below the surface for years.

Meanwhile, Christmas 1946 came and went without major incident, Mamaine making extra efforts to console Arthur and assuage his wounded pride. Things cannot have been easy, but Mamaine had, after all, rejected any possible future with Camus to stay with Arthur, and he was too relieved to punish her; indeed, he now bent over backwards to make her feel loved and appreciated. Her morale was not helped by weeks of icy weather: in February she wrote from bed, where she was staying all morning to keep warm, telling Celia that they hadn't had a bath for three weeks because all their water had to be fetched from the downstairs lavatory (which was so cold that even the soap froze) and heated on the primus, and, what with no oven and the monotony of corned beef and cold macaroni, life was wearing them down.

Arthur, however, had turned over a miraculous new leaf: 'he thinks all the time about whether I'm getting tired, or cold, or bored, and tries to remedy it by making me stay in bed & sacrificing all available stores, or thinking up some treat or cooking the dinner or whatever it is. I must say I often wonder if C., for all his niceness, would be so considerate, & rather doubt it – it is a very rare quality in men.' Nevertheless, the freezing weather continued, and their hibernation with it, and at the end of February Mamaine was 'still pretty depressed, and nearly off my head with longing to see C. As for K, he really is so sweet and affectionate and funny, I do adore him . . . alas, I now see that my nature is such that appalling conflicts are bound to occur from time to time, and K's is ditto, so I don't know how long our present matrimonial bliss will last.'

Apart from Celia, Mamaine had no one at hand to confide in, though she was never short of friends. The depth (and confusion) of her feelings for Camus, and for Arthur, were magnified by her isolation in deep-winter Wales, and by the need for discretion, for everyone's sake. Moreover, Celia had taken the plunge and moved to Paris and, with slow and unreliable post-war communications, she seemed further away than ever. Celia was determined to escape the fallout from her dead-end love affair with the philosopher Freddie Ayer, which – as she had predicted – had not ended well.

CHAPTER 10

TO PARIS AND BACK

Paris (and Camus) may have been much on Mamaine's mind throughout this winter of 1946/7, but it now became Celia's adopted home as she put the Channel between herself and the source of her unhappiness.

Freddie Ayer was another frequent contributor to *Polemic* and they had met in February 1946, only a month after she turned down George Orwell's proposal of marriage; both were instantly smitten. Freddie – whom I remember very gamely pushing me on my swing for hours as a weekend guest during our childhood – was formidably clever, at the time a fellow and dean in philosophy at Oxford and one of Britain's most prominent intellectuals. His fame, or notoriety, lay largely in being the author of the celebrated *Language, Truth and Logic*, published in the mid-1930s. In this, Ayer had introduced the

Freddie Ayer with the author, aged three

idea of Logical Positivism, the proposition that anything not verifiable by science is literally meaningless, as the world as described by science is empirically all there is. There is no room in Logical Positivism for morality, religion, beauty, God or the Absolute; it is an exhilaratingly simple but brutal refutation of anything not demonstrably and tangibly present in the here and now. Ayer's logical scepticism had galvanised and divided the philosophical world into two factions, those who embraced its ruthless clarity and those who staunchly maintained that philosophy's principal concerns remained ethics, aesthetics and metaphysics. Ayer himself had softened his stance by the mid-1940s, or he would not have contributed to *Polemic*, a journal for which ethics and aesthetics were among the central issues of debate.

The philosopher Richard Wollheim, who met Freddie around this time, described him as 'not tall, with dark wavy hair [...] He was very delicate looking, slightly swarthy, with very hooded brown eyes, and the general Modigliani cast of his face was enhanced by the two upper front teeth being slightly longer than the others. [...] But it was the movement, the constant movement, of head, hands, fingers, hair . . . this incessant movement, this constant stream of excitement, that so impressed me.'[20] He was also funny, and fond of women; Celia first met him at the offices of *Polemic* and he invited her down to Oxford almost immediately, with her boss Humphrey Slater. After George, whom she had tried but failed to find attractive enough, Celia was 'swept away' by Freddie's worldliness and *savoir faire*, and the pace of the life he led. During that first Oxford weekend they went to a party given by

Maurice Bowra ('extraordinarily witty and amusing, rather alarming I thought', wrote Celia to Mamaine), had drinks with Solly Zuckerman (a brilliant scientist and zoologist and future Chairman of the London Zoo, Zuckerman had just been appointed Companion of Honour in the New Year's honours list) and his wife, dinner with 'a nice young don called Hugh Trevor-Roper', saw two films, dined with sundry other friends, and somehow found time to spend hour upon hour talking, exploring and unravelling one another's lives.

Celia found Freddie generous and entertaining, but from the very beginning she had nagging doubts; perhaps unsurprisingly for a logical positivist, he told her he was a 'hollow man' only days after their first meeting. Nevertheless, she soon admitted to Mamaine, 'Of course Freddie is no Adonis, that's clear, but he and I have got so much in common that we feel we have known each other all our lives. [...] I left him this morning toasting his toes

Celia with Freddie Ayer and Arthur at Bwlch Ocyn

by the fire and reading a book about geometry or logic or something.' In fact, there were many things they did not share: she later claimed he was totally unmusical, had little if any appreciation of painting, and only enjoyed poetry if it was about sex. He was also quite indifferent to the countryside, and admitted that once, when staying with e.e. cummings and his wife, they suggested that he should go out for a country walk. Asked how he enjoyed it on return, all he could think of saying was, 'There are a lot of small animals and the ground is uneven.'

Moreover, he was not to be trusted, as it turned out – he used his peripatetic life between Oxford and London to keep more than one girlfriend on the go at the same time, and it swiftly dawned on Celia that, for all his protestations of passion, she was not the only one. With women, she discovered, he was 'perfidious in the extreme', and, although he genuinely loved his two children and felt real affection for a few close friends, he was 'on the whole completely indifferent and would not go a step out of his way – would not even cross the floor at a party – to see them'. Celia came to the depressing realisation that she was in an emotional *cul de sac,* and resolved to leave him, 'For I don't approve of letting oneself in for terribly long but not permanent relationships: I think them vaguely humiliating,' she wrote to Mamaine. Nevertheless, the affair continued on throughout the summer of 1946, as they had planned a holiday in the South of France together, which was predictably idyllic. Ultimately, however, she saw that the best way out was to move abroad for a while and beyond Freddie's sphere and circle. 'If only Freddie hadn't got what in Freudian circles would I imagine be called a death-wish, that is, a profound need to destroy at any costs his own happiness, there might be some hope for us; as it is there is none, as we both real-ise,' she sadly concluded, and laid plans to move on.

Like Mamaine, Celia's greatest wish at this point was to settle down in the countryside with a man she loved and have much-longed-for children, and this dream could plainly never be achieved with Freddie, however amusing and diverting he might be in the meantime. She was, in many ways, leading an enviable life, with a home in the heart of London and a role as assistant editor at *Polemic* where, thanks to Slater's wide web of connections, and her own, most of the prominent writers and artists of the day were contributors. Around her busy office days spent commissioning, chasing, editing and fine-tuning essays for the journal, she somehow found time to have almost daily lunches and dinners (and sometimes breakfasts) with girlfriends from her *Horizon* days, George Orwell, Cyril Connolly, Solly Zuckerman and Stephen Spender – that is, when she wasn't meeting up with Freddie, if in town, or attending concerts with Arthur Goodman, the man she was eventually to marry.

Arthur Goodman was not part of the intellectual circle that the twins moved in, but he had earned a strong place in their affections. He had first taken a shine to Mamaine when they found themselves stuck on a train delayed in Normandy in 1940, and was soon introduced to Celia. At that point, he was just about to embark for Singapore with his regiment, the Irish Guards, and was not seen again for five years. He was captured by the Japanese after the fall of Singapore and imprisoned in Changi for the remainder of the war. There he was bullied, beaten up and nearly starved to death, but his good fortune was to have had a pot of Marmite in his rucksack when captured: this he buried, and he and his comrades were saved from contracting beri-beri by the occasional scoops of vitamin B-rich Marmite that they managed surreptitiously to devour. Back in London, after his release, he was still so weak from his years of malnourishment that he would occasionally black out completely, but he gradually built up his strength again, joined the Foreign Office and reconnected with Celia and Mamaine, among others. That autumn, he proposed marriage to Celia, but she had not yet truly disentangled herself from Freddie and ruefully turned him down. Soon after, he met a captivating Polish aristocrat called Sofia Badeni, then studying at the Courtauld Institute, whom he swiftly married.

Despite Celia's gregarious nature, her popularity and the attractions of her work, it was all beginning to pall. Paris was a city she knew and loved from pre-war travels and would offer a change from London (the charms of which had worn thin during the years of bombing and attrition brought about by war). She also knew she could benefit from the connections Mamaine had recently made, so she began to make enquiries about finding a job there.

Mamaine was delighted to hear of this plan: 'When I arrived back here this afternoon after a harrowing outing (during which I ditched the car or got it stuck in the mud three times) Arthur yelled out "Good news!" and gave me your telegram. Twinnie, I can't say how delighted and overjoyed I am . . . it is simply wonderful and I am sure will solve all your problems.' She advised Celia to settle near the Boulevard Saint-Germain: 'Camus told me he knew of lots of nice cheap hotels there, but I think it would be better if you could avoid meeting him really, especially as I am terribly obsessed by him and if I knew you might see him couldn't resist sending direct or indirect messages, which would be most unfair if he is supposed to be forgetting about me. I do seem to be rather in love with him, blast it.'

Alas, Paris was not to fulfil its promise. The city was still licking its wounds and dealing with the long hangover of war. Early spring of 1947, when Celia arrived, was freezing – even the coal barges were icebound – and her morale was understandably low, both missing Freddie and determined to forget him. She did contact Camus and Francine but had to walk on eggshells on Mamaine's behalf, and she hankered for her wider social circle and the familiarity of London. Like all cities, Paris can be achingly lonely, all the more so in deep midwinter and in the aftermath of an enemy occupation that had made its citizens more than usually wary of one another. Isaiah Berlin recalled the frozen city, at this time, being 'empty and hollow and dead, like an exquisite corpse'.

Celia soon succumbed to various chest infections exacerbated by her chronic asthma. She was admitted to hospital, causing much anxiety to Mamaine, who was holed up in Wales with Arthur and at the mercy of an uncertain postal system. 'Darling Twinnie, I was absolutely in despair to hear that you are still ill and have had such an appalling time,' wrote Mamaine in March. 'What <u>on earth</u> is wrong with you? If only I could come over and go away with you – I would give anything to, but for financial and other reasons it is quite impossible.' Camus came to the rescue and arranged for a private room for Celia in the hospital.

When she was discharged various friends rallied to have her to stay, but the effort of relegating Freddie to the past and trying to make a success of her new job took a toll on her recovery.

Her role as editorial assistant on the trilingual monthly periodical *Occident* turned out to be disappointing; it brought her into contact with a wide range of writers and thinkers, as *Polemic* had done in London, but it was a ropey set-up, so seriously underfunded that bills were rarely paid, and she quickly realised that she must extricate herself and find another job as soon as possible. Mamaine recommended asking Camus's publisher Gaston Gallimard – 'all-powerful, and able and willing to take you on at any time', she suggested hopefully – but it was not as simple as that.

Mamaine went on to distract Celia from her woes by telling her that 'believe it or not, K now has only one interest: mysticism. He also believes in miracles. There is a man called Dr Rhein in Duke University, US, who has demonstrated that if one is throwing dice and wants a six to turn up, it will do so by a significant proportion above the laws of probability; thus proving the influence of mind over matter.' It is interesting to learn that Arthur's interest in the realm beyond the senses and science, that of coincidence and parapsychology, stretched back as far as 1947, though it would be many years before this took shape in his writings.

In March 1947, Mamaine asked Celia to send her the leading articles that Camus was writing in *Combat* – revealing thereby that she must have been in touch with him. Camus had also written to tell her how he had been teased by Sartre and de Beauvoir on his return from Avignon, and had denied going there with Mamaine, but feared he had given himself away on another occasion by his tone of voice in discussing her. Meanwhile, Mamaine was sleeping badly, able to think of little other than her craving to be with Camus, and having recurrent nightmares about trying frantically to arrange a rendezvous with him and not being able to, or only for a moment.

Mamaine could not help confiding in Celia once again about Arthur's black moods – the inevitable result of writer's block, combined with his drinking – which led to accesses of regret and remorse. Their relative solitude made Mamaine's struggles against Arthur's overwhelming cynicism and pessimism often hard to sustain. 'He bewailed the collapse of his heroes, and said how awful it was to have nobody to look up to,' she wrote. 'However, I will say one thing for K: he has more moral courage than anyone I have ever met. As a rule, when one objects to his statements on politics etc. one finds afterwards that one's objections are based on purely conventional ways of thinking and on a cowardly refusal to face the facts of the situation.' It was this faith in the core of him, the essential seriousness of the man, that kept Mamaine onside, despite the daily battle to keep her spirits up.

She and Arthur were becoming 'obsessed' by how awful the weather was in Wales; one evening, she related, 'there was a 90-mile-an-hour gale, and as we were frying our dinner on the sitting room fire there was a loud crash, and half the big 17th century west window fell in on us, followed by lashings of rain. But we are well off compared with most parts of England, where people are rowing to their local pubs in boats.' As a result, they endlessly discussed where else they might live, dreaming of escape to Palestine, to Provence, to California – any place where the weather would cease to be the constant enemy. Mamaine was advocating Europe on the grounds that 'as there probably remain only a few years in which life in Europe will be possible, one should make the best of them'.

She loved France and Italy, spoke both languages well, plus German, and was well-read in European literature. Koestler, however, was a terrible linguist and spoke even English with a strong Hungarian accent to the end of his life; for him, the prospect of living in a country where he could not easily communicate was anathema. More important, he was convinced it was only a matter of months until the Communists got into power in France, a prospect he couldn't abide. Mamaine secretly longed to return to Paris, and even harboured dreams of living in Provence after her transformative time there with Camus. Failing that, she fantasised about going off by herself to stay in a small hotel there for a month or two: 'I have got a 1947 Michelin which has a map of isolated hotels,' she told Celia. 'It is all I can do not to gloat over it all day.'

She was determined at least to visit Paris for a weekend in April to see Celia, though she confessed to being nervous about it: how could she spend time in the city without seeing Camus? Yet she refused to deceive Arthur a second time. She did manage to get to Paris and back without succumbing to temptation, and returned home in early May to sunny weather, at long last, and the delivery of a new piano, an upright Bechstein which I still own; finally, she could get back to her playing, which she had sorely missed. This helped to dispel the gloom brought on by Arthur's renewed depression, or 'anxiety neurosis', as they both called it. Arthur's phase of devoted attentiveness (and relative sobriety) had lasted no more than a couple of months before he again fell prey to dark thoughts and irascibility. 'Poor K is in despair,' Mamaine wrote to Celia, 'his brain is simply not functioning at all, and he still can't get back into his work; it is now over 2 months since he was working properly, so you can imagine the state he's in, and how impossible he is.'

He would be morose all day, then a wild glint would come into his eye at the prospect of alcohol and company, and he would stay up half the night drinking heavily with whichever of their neighbours he could corral into dinner. The following day would, predictably, be spent in acute remorse and the nursing of a hangover. 'He is always begging me to stop him drinking,' Mamaine told Celia, 'but I'm damned if I'm going to act nursemaid to someone of 42.' They now had rows about even the simplest things, such as whether to go to the Oakley Arms, where Arthur was prepared to talk to any old bore in order to prop up the bar for a couple of hours, but which Mamaine resisted with all her strength, longing simply to stay at home in front of the fire with a novel and her music.

Arthur's depressions were genuine, and his prevailing blackness of mood was difficult to withstand, even for someone of her essentially positive temperament. Both she and Celia had been prone to anxiety from an early age, with the onset of their father's mortal illness, and descended into regular depressions or '*cafards*', as they called them. Anxiety was hovering in the wings for both of them, waiting to pounce, and they feared and dreaded its renewed onslaught. The often restless quality of their lives can be attributed to this, I believe, and Mamaine would resort to flippancy to protect herself and pre-empt any breach in her defences. Now she confessed to Celia, 'I fear for myself, living with K – his cynicism and pessimism are so overwhelming, and besides he has such *mauvais caractère* that he brings out all mine too.' Additionally, she was desperately anxious about Celia, who had been in and out of hospital again with, among other things, a collapsed lung, and with whom she longed to be in closer contact. 'Dear Twinnie,' she wrote in late May, 'I haven't heard from you since the letter I had from the Hospital, so I am worried if you are dead or alive. Please let me know at once – with details, if the latter.'

Volatile as ever, Arthur's spirits picked up as the creative juices started to flow again, to Mamaine's profound relief. 'Everything is very *paisible*,' she wrote to Celia in June. 'K's brain seems to have regained some of its former properties, in any case he is writing a missing chapter of his book at great speed which gives me some time off. But I do not feel as *paisible* as I might myself: my obsession about C[amus] gets worse and worse. However, obsessions do have the advantage that they make one think . . . Whether it gets one anywhere, is another question.'

As spring thawed Paris out and her health improved, Celia started to enjoy life in Paris more and made new friends, including the artist and model Isobel Rawsthorne, the journalist Gita Sereny and her photographer husband

Don Honeyman, and the writer Romain Gary and his wife
Lesley Blanch, author of *The Wilder Shores of Love*. Romain
Gary was a dashing and wilfully eccentric figure whose
origins were swathed in mystery and who became a celebrated pilot during the war with the Free French. Mamaine
plainly considered him wildly indiscreet and unreliable,
hence her advice to Celia, who was off to dine with Gary:
'Take my advice and maintain a mysterious silence about
everything.' To Mamaine, stewing in Wales with an irascible and unpredictable Arthur, reports of Celia's growing
circle of friends now provided a welcome distraction: 'I
enjoy more than anything hearing about your colourful
life,' she wrote in June, 'so do tell me about it as often as
you get a chance.'

There were, meanwhile, amusing accounts in Mamaine's
letters of various people who passed through Bwlch Ocyn:
Arthur's mother, Adela, for one, with whom they had an
extraordinary conversation about Freud. Both Mamaine
and Arthur ascribed most of his worst neuroses to his
mother, who had given him scant affection as a child,
smothering him instead with endless selfish demands, and
no love was lost between them as a result. They both found
her maddening, egotistic, extremely stupid and hopelessly
neurotic, and they dreaded her visits – which, though fortunately rare, were not rare enough. During one of them,
Adela spotted various volumes by Freud ('that Dr Freund',
as she referred to him) on their shelves, and volunteered, 'I
used to know him very well when I was 17.' 'How did you
come to meet him?' asked Arthur, somewhat surprised.
'Well, he was great friends with Tante Lore, and very proud
to be able to frequent our family, and one day Tante Lore

sent me to him, as I had a nervous tic.' 'So what did he do?' 'He massaged the back of my neck and asked a lot of annoying questions – anyway he was a revolting man with a black beard – *sehr unsympathisen* – so I stopped going to see him.'* 'The idea of how different Arthur's and consequently my life would have been had his mother not stopped going to Freud is extremely fascinating,' remarked Mamaine to Celia.

Later in June, Celia managed to get over to London from Paris to consult various doctors, and to Mamaine's joy she made plans to visit them in Wales. It was unadulterated happiness for the twins to be together again, and at last to be able to discuss their lives and dilemmas at length and in depth; to roam the Welsh hills and watch birds on the shoreline; to unburden themselves in total confidence. Celia and Arthur had grown fond of each other, too, so harmony – one supposes – prevailed. After they had seen her off on the train back to London, Mamaine and Arthur went for a long drive to Anglesey and stopped off at Red Wharf Bay, 'the place where somebody deposited the remains of his wife whom he had murdered because she had nagged him – no more legs etc. were to be seen sticking out of the sand, but it was very pretty'. The weather was hot and they had many enjoyable times over the ensuing weeks, but 'I am filled with nostalgia and obsessions', Mamaine wrote to Celia after her twin's departure.

Celia returned to her life in Paris and her job at *Occident,* which was still struggling along thanks largely to her efforts and contacts, and was in the end preferable to various proffered openings at UNESCO or the

* 'very unpleasant'

British Council. Her health continued to be fragile, causing Mamaine more anguish – one of her letters confesses, 'I dreamed last night that you were in a nursing home, the owners of which were secretly poisoning you, so that you became iller and iller without suspecting the cause; also they hid you; but I managed to discover you and was about to call the police in to liberate you, but uncertain whether I should be in time . . .'

Meanwhile, George Orwell and Celia continued to correspond, his letters always addressed to 'Dearest Celia'. In October 1947 he wrote to her from Jura of another marvellous summer – 'six weeks without a drop of rain, and we went for some wonderful picnics on the other side of the island, which is quite uninhabited but where there is an empty shepherd's cottage one can sleep in. It is a beautiful coast, green water and white sand, and a few miles inland lochs full of trout which never get fished because they're too far from anywhere.' Celia had evidently asked him to write for *Occident*, which was similar in focus to *Polemic*, as he continues, 'I will write for you when I can. I certainly would like some French francs.' Knowing her fondness for Richard, he included news of his little son in almost every letter: how fast he was growing, how sturdy he was, 'most enterprising and full of energy & out working on the farm all day long', how he didn't see enough of other children (he was not yet at school) so was backward in talking, how he loved practical tasks but didn't show much enthusiasm for learning to read. 'I think he is going to grow up to be a practical man, an engineer or something like that,' George observed, presciently.[21]

Sadly this was followed by a letter in December reporting that he'd been so ill that he'd been told he would have to go to a sanatorium for four months, near Glasgow – in fact, Hairmyres Hospital in East Kilbride. He ended on a poignant note, 'I would love to see you some time – but heaven knows when that will happen. With much love George.'

Celia and George's letters were overshadowed by his deteriorating health, as tuberculosis was diagnosed and took an ever-tighter grip on him. 'It is TB, which of course was bound to get me sooner or later, in fact I've had it before, though not so badly,' he admitted in January 1948, adding defiantly, 'However I don't think it is very serious, & I seeming [sic] to be getting better slowly.' His stiff upper lip was to the fore: 'The winter of 1946–7 in London was really a bit too thick, & I think it was probably what started me on this show.' He continues, poignantly in view of what was to come, 'If I'm cured and about by then, as I assume I shall be, I am going to try to wangle a correspondent's job this winter so as to winter in a warm place.'

In March 1948 he was sympathising with Celia's own health setbacks, trading news on available drugs and telling her, 'I am much better, though it will inevitably be a good long time before I am out of bed,' which didn't sound encouraging but was plainly an improvement on 'feeling like death' as he had reported before. He had now decided to make his permanent home in Jura, as 'It's a good place for Richard to grow up in, especially if the bombs start dropping before long,' expressing his grave concerns about the atom bomb, and the deep pessimism he was articulating in his novel-in-progress. He finished, 'I wish I was with you in Paris, I wonder if they have put Marshal Ney's statue back outside the Closerie des Lilas – but I dare say the Germans melted him down to get the bronze.' In May, still in hospital, weak and thin and only able to get up for two hours each day, he concluded a chattier letter trading news of mutual friends with:

> How I wish I was with you in Paris, now that spring is there. Do you ever go to the Jardin des Plantes? I used to love it, though there was really nothing of interest except the rats, which at one time overran it & were so tame that they would almost eat out of your hand. In the end they got to be such a nuisance that they introduced cats & more or less wiped them out.

Echoes of *Down and Out in Paris and London* lived on in his troubled mind. He sent her a reprint of his novel *Coming Up for Air*, which conjured for Celia overwhelming memories of the twins' childhood in Melton. 'It is clear,' she wrote to Mamaine, 'that George has exactly what we have, ie a nostalgia not for his childhood as such, but for that particular kind of life which can be had, more or less, at any age, & which I suppose he <u>does</u> have up to a point on Jura – though it always changes a lot & becomes more difficult after each war.'

Mamaine, meanwhile, thought constantly of Paris, and the two people she cared about most: Celia and Camus. She loved France, she told Edmund Wilson, 'in spite of all its rot and corruption', and longed to live there, but shared Arthur's fear that it would shortly become a Soviet satellite, 'and the best people one knows won't survive'. Everything hinged upon de Gaulle's ability to crush the Communist fifth column and win over the left, but there was a fear that his aggressive tactics might drive those hitherto undecided in their loyalties into the Communist camp instead. Koestler, too, was determined to revisit the city where arguments still raged between the left and the right, unresolved. He felt too far from the action in north Wales, and wanted to be back in the fight, to weigh in and influence people.

So, at the start of October 1947, they travelled back to Paris and reconnected immediately with André Malraux – now *chef de propaganda* of de Gaulle's RPF (*Rassemblement du Peuple Français*) party – and his wife Madeleine over vodka and blinis at the Plaza Athenée Hotel. Malraux admitted he was running a huge risk 'in using his reputation as a man of the Left to help the reactionaries', and rose considerably in Mamaine and Arthur's estimation as a result. The following morning at the Café des Deux Magots they were happily reunited with Simone de Beauvoir, any past acrimony apparently dissolved, and friendships re-established as paramount over political misalignments. As de Beauvoir wrote to Nelson Algren, her sometime lover, 'I do not remember what you think about him [Koestler] as a writer; I believe I told you what a strange night we spent with him, Sartre and Camus, everybody being drunk and crying about friendship and political discrepancies; it was very funny. I like him and he has a very pretty sweet wife; we went together to an exhibition [...]'.[22]

Sadly, this truce was not to last. Dinner a week later with Sartre and de Beauvoir at the Camuses' new flat in the rue Séguier started warmly, the guests enjoying lobster, chicken and champagne brought by Arthur and Mamaine, and Francine's delicious cooking. However, the arrival of Harold Kaplan of *Partisan Review*, a friend of Arthur's suspected by Sartre and de Beauvoir of being an American spy, lit the blue touch paper, and a blazing row about liberty erupted between Koestler and Sartre, fuelled by quantities of brandy. Mamaine noted, 'K got so cross that he let fly at Sartre and said who are you to talk about liberty, when for years you've run a magazine [*Les Temps Modernes*] which was *communisant,* and thus condoned the deportations of millions of people from the Baltic States and so on?', following which he and Mamaine stormed out, Koestler muttering darkly, 'Now we are enemies'. An apologetic letter served to mend fences, at least temporarily, but such outbursts were to become an ever more frequent and, for Mamaine, regrettable part of Koestler's repertoire.

De Beauvoir continued to have mixed feelings about Koestler, as she later explained to Algren: 'Koestler is a strange, interesting man; sometimes when he is drunk, he is very conceited and he feels a kind of martyr, and he takes himself so seriously it is awful. But last Tuesday he was very sincere, and simple and friendly.'[23] A few days later, she sums up their political antipathy in a nutshell: 'What is rather wrong with him is that he hates communists so much he can be friends with the most conservative people and write in conservative papers and support a conservative policy, like the people of *Partisan Review*.'[24] Their friendship would always be contingent and compromised by ideology because Koestler, unlike Camus, would always prioritise political alignment over friendship.

Back in Wales for the onset of another winter, Mamaine immersed herself in a steady routine of work and domestic life, and managed to achieve a degree of harmony that soothed her troubled mind. 'As I have no desires,' she was able to tell Celia, 'I am having a rest from my usual mental & moral struggles.' However, Arthur's general irascibility returned, and tempers became badly frayed. 'Yesterday we had a shouting match,' reported Mamaine, 'and I threw a saucepan full of mashed potato at a wall, but for one thing I disapprove of this sort of thing, and secondly it wears one out emotionally and gives one a headache.' She did have moments of feeling quite gay and happy, she wrote, but they were usually scotched by some new row. She confessed that she was desperately worried about her future life with Arthur but was 'determined to make a success of it if it's humanly possible'.

Recounting how an amusing dinner with friends ended, as always, with her trying in vain to persuade Arthur to leave at midnight, she admitted that a part of her sympathised with him: 'he simply has an Eastern constitution, like Russians, Hungarians and Slavs always do, which makes him not only able, but anxious, to stay up ALL night once he gets going,' she told Celia. She, however, suffered torments of exhaustion after midnight, like Rubashov (in *Darkness at Noon*) after several weeks of interrogation. 'In vain I think of T. E. Lawrence and remember his endurance as he paced the desert on his camel for days without sleep (but he suffered hell doing it); there always comes a time when I feel I just can't stick it any longer.'

Through Arthur's current book-in-progress, *Insight and Outlook,* on which they were both working so hard, she was introduced to his theory of the twin planes of the Tragic and the Trivial, which helped her to place her confused emotions into some larger context. Koestler's argument was that we all move to and fro between the Tragic, consisting of ultimate and irreducible truths, and the Trivial, concerned with everyday life. Occasionally people are forced to live for long periods on the Tragic plane – for example, fighter pilots in war – and, in order to ease the strain, they project the trivial onto the tragic: joking about the death of friends or making light of fatal accidents, and thus drawing death's sting. The artist, Koestler argued, lives on the line of intersection between the two planes but, instead of projecting the trivial onto the tragic, he sees the trivial in the light of the tragic – of the underlying realities of experience. 'This interlacing of the Tragic and the Trivial planes is implicit in all great works of art; it is the ultimate quality of the creative mind by means of which it is able to transcend the narrow limits of the self,' he concluded.[25] Mamaine certainly embraced the idea that it was this ability to see things in terms of their deeper, more archetypal significance that could redeem the more difficult aspects of life, rendering it bearable on a day-to-day level. 'On the Tragic plane K and I always get on admirably – it is only the Trivial plane which sometimes gets us down,' she wryly remarked to Celia.

As they drew towards the finish of his ambitious project – which sought to cover 'art, humour, discovery and invention, the influence of emotion on thought, mysticism and ethics' – they both worked almost night and day, literally dreaming about the book when their fevered minds allowed them to sleep, and finding a renewed harmony in their joint dedication to the cause. They managed to pack up the final typescript for the publisher just before Christmas, and had a celebratory dinner 'with our 1916 claret from Llandudno Junction'. Richard and Zita Crossman were due for Christmas and were bringing a turkey to accompany their goose, so they were able at last to relax and enjoy some respite from their Stakhanovite labours.

CHAPTER 11

ESCAPE

New Year 1948 brought long-delayed plans for travel to Europe, and later, for Arthur, to America. Mamaine was never happier than when in France or Italy, and wherever she went, either with Arthur or alone, she found herself in the midst of things: her warm and open nature, near-perfect French and passable Italian and German made most new encounters a delight. *Insight and Outlook* completed and delivered, she persuaded Arthur to drive down through the Midi to Italy, where they had various friends to visit.

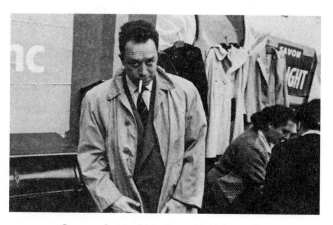

Camus at the Marché aux Puces, Paris's flea market

En route, they spent a few weeks in Paris, to see Celia and to catch up with their friends. The latter was hazardous, given that emotions between them all had run so high. Their first reunion dinner with Celia and the Camuses passed without incident, but a few days later the five of them were joined by Sartre and de Beauvoir, and the evening turned into another alcohol-fuelled marathon as they progressed from a Creole bistro to a Spanish nightclub, and then to a Russian *boîte* where they were plied with vodka.

By Mamaine's admission in her diary, all got very drunk:

> including me, as I had been feeling gloomy & felt it was my best hope of cheering up: it worked splendidly. Camus (also fairly drunk, which he rarely is) suddenly started to talk to me with great intensity of feeling […] I asked him if he was happy & he said 'No, desperately unhappy – I've been unhappy since we parted.' I asked him why and he said, 'because I have nothing I want – I wanted so much to live with you, and we couldn't, and now there's nothing left for me.' He & I & Sartre & the Castor [de Beauvoir] went out so that I could let them into the car to get some things, & in the street Camus kept grabbing my arms & talking in this sense & taking no notice of the other two (who wandered ahead). I said, 'We can't talk like this here' & he said 'I must say these things now while I'm drunk enough to be able to' & held onto me and said he'd wept all night when I left, & that he thought all the time of me, & of Avignon, and of how happy we'd been there, he'd

never been so happy before or since & he was in despair. […] I said 'I doubt whether you're capable of loving really, because you go with so many women and that corrupts one's feelings in a way, I think' & he said '*Tu viens de dire ma condamnation*'.* Only once before have I seen C in such a state. I was very moved, too. We then went back to the *boîte* and after a while succeeded in getting out K, who was so drunk he could hardly stand, and very recalcitrant. When C tried to make him get into the car, he let fly, leaving C with a black eye. K then wandered off; C got into the driving seat & Sartre, Simone & I also got into the car, & C sat with his face in his hands saying: '*Quel con! de faire ça à un type qui essaie de l'aider!* I was longing to knock him down; it was for your sake that I didn't (he said to me), but you can tell him that it's finished between us', etc.†
He was wild. I told him not to take it so seriously, K was too drunk to know what he was doing; & C drove us back to our hotel *à toute vitesse*. Here, the Sartres wandered off and C made another impassioned speech, saying that he'd always desired me more than I had him, & so on. Then he went off and I joined the others. My hangover was so bad I had to stay in bed <u>all</u> the next day (today).

Camus had to wear dark glasses for some time while his black eye wore off, and his relations with Koestler reached their nadir.

---

* 'You have just announced my damnation.'

† 'What an idiot! to do that to a guy who was trying to help him!'

Arthur and Mamaine spent a few weeks more in Paris, seeing Celia, mending political bridges (where broken), dining frequently with Sartre and Malraux but avoiding Camus, before setting off for the south. Arthur's reputation opened doors wherever they went, but occasionally his past caught up with them, not altogether to Mamaine's delight: arriving in a small hotel near Nice, they discovered that the *patronne*, a Turkish princess, was an old acquaintance of his, or more, and they had to have lunch with her and her unsavoury young lover 'while with great *tu-toi*-ings she discussed with K her past'. In Florence they dined with, among others, Bernard Berenson at his splendid home in the Tuscan hills, I Tatti. He was then eighty-two but 'very smart and charming', though unfortunately Arthur had a fit of aphasia and 'kept talking about Piero della Francesca when he meant Simone Martini etc, with the result that his conversation was quite unintelligible'. Mamaine was almost

I Tatti, Bernard Berenson's house in the Tuscan hills

struck dumb by the loveliness of I Tatti, set amid the hills near Settignano above Florence, its formal terraces of topiary designed by two young Englishmen, Cecil Pinsent and Geoffrey Scott, falling away down the hillside into fields of wildflowers and blossoming almond trees, bounded by tumbling hedges of wisteria. She was overawed, too, by the quality of Berenson's collection of masterpieces of the early Sienese School and High Renaissance. Despite Arthur's artistic *faux pas*, their encounter gave rise to a warm, if brief, correspondence, with Berenson sending Mamaine a reproduction of his Domenico Veneziana *Madonna*, which she had particularly admired, and conversing with Arthur about the fate of Europe.

No sooner had they arrived in Rome and installed themselves, after a long search, in a very civilised hotel, 'than K announced that he loathed Italy passionately and had always known he wouldn't like coming here, but I had dragged him, and so on. Actually of course he enjoys himself madly most of the time.' As for herself, Mamaine confessed to Celia, 'I don't know if this letter conveys how much I am enjoying myself: the whole trip is just bliss for me and I wish it would go on for months.' She still asked after Camus, but told Celia that when she returned to stay with her in Paris she would rather not see him more than strictly necessary; 'indeed I would rather not see him at all'. Having achieved some measure of equilibrium, she knew it would be madness to place it again under threat. And in reality, Arthur was, despite his complaints, in excellent spirits, as they drove around the *campagna* visiting ruins and gardens and dining with friends and acquaintances.

They ran into difficulties on their drive back up through Italy, since, despite the cold and deep snow, Arthur insisted on crossing the pass between Florence and Bologna without chains on the car. All too predictably they got stuck, causing a lengthy tailback on the narrow mountain road. Mamaine went to get ropes from a peasant's house on the roadside, and, while the men tackled the ropes, she sat by the fire with the lady of the house eating pieces of rabbit cooked in oil. Further on, they were again delayed by drifting snow so had lunch in a mountain hut, 'consisting of sausages obviously made of cat', before breasting the pass and careering headlong down the other side, since the ropes made their brakes seize up. In a café in Parma they heard what they thought was the radio broadcasting opera, only to discover it was one workman outside singing Verdi arias to another, softly, in such a lovely voice 'that K and I both nearly wept, it was so beautiful and moving, and swallowed our grappas quickly and rushed out; and as we left the workers pressed their noses against the glass door and waved at us'.

This elegiac note was broken by a spell in Milan, which she loathed: 'We went to some parties of intellectuals which were pure suffering for me,' she groaned. From there (leaving Arthur to make his own way back to Paris) she went on solo to Trieste, which she found fascinating: 'a curious mixture of Italians, Slovenes and relics of the Austro-Hungarian empire'. She was the guest there of Bob and Jane Joyce, an American diplomat and his wife who lived in an expansive and elegant flat in the Austro-Hungarian style: 'my bedroom contains a large white porcelain stove and a portrait of Franz Josef, and the salon next door has a painted ceiling, furniture upholstered in crimson silk, chandelier, gilt mirrors and all the rest; and an open fire which is always blazing away.' There was also a grand piano, which, much to her delight, made her sound like Rachmaninov.

She was immediately whisked off by the Joyces to a string of parties and balls, with Prince this and Princess that, for all the world as if the Austro-Hungarian empire had never foundered. But beneath all the froth she made some real friendships, too, with Cyrus Sulzberger, lead foreign correspondent of the *New York Times* and his Greek wife Marina, and with an Italian diplomat called Gastone Giudotti. 'While the Sulzbergers were here we went out quite a bit to the local nightclub,' she wrote to Arthur in America. 'You would have laughed to see me driving round Trieste in a topolino with five men, mostly Hungarians, hanging on all over it and singing "*boci boci tarka*". Now however we lead a quieter life . . .'

Picnic in the hills near Duino with Bob and Jane Joyce,
Cy and Marina Sulzberger, and Gastone Giudotti

With Gastone and the Joyces, she spent leisurely days driving along the coast to Duino and Venice, and into the lush foothills of the Giulian Alps for lunches and picnics.

The castle of Duino on its rocky fastness particularly entranced them: Mamaine had always loved the poetry of Rilke, and his Elegies, written there, seemed to echo off the walls. The only signs of political ferment were bloodcurdling Communist

Mamaine flanked by Marina (left) and Jane and Bob Joyce (right) in the Piazza San Marco, Venice

posters in all the villages denouncing the horrors of American imperialism, one accusing Truman of having claimed during the war that he would like as many people killed as possible. To counteract this the Demo-Christians displayed stark photos of emaciated corpses in the crevasses into which the Yugoslav partisans had thrown their victims when they had attempted to take Trieste eighteen months before.

In the midst of all this she found time to read *Oedipus Rex* in an Italian translation lent to her by Gastone, go to a boxing match, and simply to enjoy herself 'in a carefree, physical sort of way', which was indeed far removed from her life in Wales. 'In Trieste life is much simpler & nobody takes it *en tragique*, they are too busy trying to survive while at the same time enjoying themselves as much as possible – & seem to succeed well in both. It is easier there because of the sun & the sea, the corso onto the piazza, the flower market by the canal, & all the other delights of provincial life.' She left Trieste for Paris with a heavy heart, overnighting in Milan where she witnessed an ugly pre-election scene, described graphically to Arthur:

The whole piazza was filled with men, mostly pretty awful-looking young communists, you know the type. From time to time a man would break way from a group & the whole group would run after him as he dodged from side to side, & people from all over the piazza would rush after him, & they all beat the man who was running, or knocked him down, and kicked him. This happened about once a minute. I saw the crowd rush at private cars driving round the piazza & break the windows & leap on the roof. It was a disgusting sight. Later, when I'd had dinner & returned to the piazza, it was still going on, but soldiers on trucks had appeared & were pointing guns in the air, or at the crowd, & police with truncheons in jeeps. I heard afterwards some people had been taken to hospital after being hit by the police, who nevertheless looked pretty ineffectual.

It's the same most nights there – one night the Communists beat people up, the next night it's the Demo-Christians – what savages! & what cowards they are.

Back in Paris, Arthur was called on by Malraux to help find 'between ten and fifteen million francs' for the Gaullistes' anti-Communist propaganda, and went to his old friend Guy de Rothschild to ask if he could stump up the money. Intrigued but unconvinced, de Rothschild invited Arthur and Mamaine to dinner with Malraux and his wife, where they watched, fascinated, as he set out his stall. 'Malraux was more extraordinary than ever,' Mamaine reported to Celia. 'He spoke for four hours non-stop. Usual brilliance.' It was clear, however, that he had abandoned any former left-wing sympathies to move to the right alongside de Gaulle, leaving Koestler both dismayed and disillusioned. Cue more frustration on his part, and more rows with Mamaine. Both were relieved when he set off alone on a lecture tour to the United States, to be lionised once more from coast to coast as he championed his message of *Pax Americana*, which drew enthusiastic press and adoring crowds. Seen off from New York with parties given by Mary McCarthy and Hannah Arendt, he wrote to Mamaine: 'Five times a day I am telling myself this is a country where I want to be forever, five times a day that I would rather be dead than live here.'

From Paris, Mamaine wrote to Arthur that she had once seen Camus, 'who looked extremely chirpy and said he'd heard you were drinking like a fish, which I denied'. Arthur didn't rise to this, replying instead that 'I read your letter [about the demonstration] to various Senators and State Department people, who all say you should be a journalist; this made me very proud. There are various legends about you circulating here, all very flattering [...]. Very much love from your loving and homesick spouse.'

Mamaine stayed on in Paris with Celia for several weeks, and then brought the Camuses over to London for a visit, taking them to various parties, *Horizon*'s included, to the National Gallery, to the Prospect of Whitby in the docklands for lunch ('which Camus adored'), to Windsor and Eton, and to lunch in the House of Commons. She spent every day in their company until they left for Scotland, 'leaving me very lonely and sad. It has been so nice having Camus about, though sad for me, in some ways. He really is the nicest man on earth,' she added, with more than a touch of wistfulness.

By late May both Mamaine and Arthur were back in Wales, Arthur plainly rattled by the Camuses' visit and 'in the worst possible mood' – nothing she could do was right. Just spotting a pile of books that had been on the same chair for three days prompted him to claim it was impossible to live with someone so untidy: 'At this

Camus, London

I simply collapsed with laughter, but of course it is quite true, it is exactly this kind of thing which will get us down in the long run. Because I just don't notice piles of books, and never will […] I do sometimes wonder if I live with K because I want to, or because I'm too cowardly to leave him – which I certainly am, owing to my terror of living alone,' she confided to Celia, to whom she just had to let off steam. 'Wales is more awful than ever, the climate drains my vitality, the problem of running the house efficiently is insuperable […]. But don't think I am unhappy,' she added, more brightly. 'For it is nice to be in the country and I want to read some books and do some work for a change.'

I do not have Celia's letters to Mamaine from this period – indeed, owing to Mamaine's peripatetic life and frequent moves and travels, many fewer of Celia's letters have survived – but I gather that she was struggling with both

Camus with Francine on their trip to London

her health and her job. 'Everybody here is very concerned here about your health,' Mamaine wrote to Celia, 'and Humphrey [Slater] is very much in favour of your not doing a job at all, but just living and possibly collecting English books and reading them for a French publisher, supervising the translations and so on. I am coming round to the idea of your not working myself. Humphrey also thinks you should marry X; but although I told him I thought this quite a good idea, I see it is quite impossible […]' To and fro went the letters, with encouragement and advice – not always taken – gossip about friends, and requests for (rationed) clothes, food and favourite books.

Nothing was off-limits, and the tone veers from the tragic to the trivial and back again. Their correspondence was the backbone of their lives, the repository of their thoughts and deepest feelings, and it steeled them both for the tougher times they encountered. A later letter to Celia empathises:

> I am terribly sorry you are having such a hellish time with flats jobs etc. Yes there is no getting away from it, life is hell most of the time, and personally I think it is best to realise that and not expect much, but simply concentrate on what one thinks is right in any given circumstances, I mean ethically right, not right from the point of view of expediency.
>
> Could you please send some <u>coffee</u> soonest? We can't get any here and life is even more hell without it . . .

CHAPTER 12

THE PROMISED LAND

In May 1948, the British Mandate for Palestine was finally terminated, and the independent State of Israel declared, with David Ben-Gurion as prime minister. The fate of Palestine had been an obsession of Arthur's ever since his first visit there twenty years before, stoked by his resolute Zionism, and he had distilled his ideas on it into his 1946 novel *Thieves in the Night*. At the news of Israel's independence from the British (brought about in the wake of terrorist attacks by the Jewish Irgun and Haganah networks, including the bombing of the King David Hotel in Jerusalem) he determined to be in the thick of it as soon as possible.

Dick Wyndham, Mamaine's former lover, had for the last three years been reporting from Jerusalem on the Arab–Israeli conflict, embedded with the Arab Forces as Special Representative of the *Sunday Times*. Arthur and Mamaine were not to meet up with Dick as planned, however, for in mid-May, while covering a skirmish in the desert between Israeli troops and the Arab League, he stood up in a trench in his Arab League uniform to get a photograph and was instantly hit by a sniper's bullet. It is not known why he took such foolhardy action, but his half-brother Francis told Celia years later that he was still depressed and half-inclined to death after the end of his affair with Mamaine. His obituary in the *Sunday Times* was written by Ian Fleming, who described him as:

> [...] one of the great Bohemian figures of his age. Disdainful of the conventions, he moved arrogantly through the artistic circles of his time, a fine, careless figure, larger and more varied than the life around him. With one foot in White's Club and the other in Bloomsbury, he aloofly bestrode both worlds – collecting friends, smiting his critics, going his own quixotic way.
>
> On the other side of his character he was a hard-working craftsman, an experienced amateur airman and navigator, and a foreign correspondent in the highest tradition. By his death the foreign service of Kemsley Newspapers has lost a fine representative, but the real tributes to his memory will come from those friends and admirers who saw in his insolent but gentle brilliance those qualities of 'panache' and chivalry which are the inheritance of great Englishmen.[26]

There is no record of Mamaine's reaction to Dick's death, but it must have been a bitter loss. Dick hovered as a huge figure in her life, even when absent: her first and arguably deepest love, whose charisma and deeply cultured nature had opened all doors to her and Celia, and set them on their adult path. She owed him so much, profoundly regretted that they had not been able to fix and preserve the happiness they had found together, and felt uneasy guilt at having thrown her lot in with Arthur, despite Dick's long absences abroad. He would have been no easier a companion in life, but it was in her nature always to overlook entrenched human failings in favour of the bigger picture, and her unwavering belief in Dick and in his courage and integrity long outlasted her physical affair with him. The knowledge of his love and unceasing regard was precious to her, and she guarded it closely, fending off enquiries and jealousies from Arthur and others. Now that this bedrock, a deep seam in her emotional life, was gone, it threw Arthur – and her volatile relationship with him – into ever starker relief. Both were about to be severely tested.

Dick Wyndham, 1948. 'A war correspondent of more advanced years, whose rugged features express years of wisdom', as one Arab newspaper put it

Arthur had managed to get commissions from the *Manchester Guardian, New York Herald Tribune* and *Le Figaro* to report on the developing situation in Israel, and he and Mamaine arrived in Haifa on 4 June after a two-day relay of chartered flights across the Mediterranean and Cyprus. After a few days' rest on Mount Carmel, with the enchanting sound of turtle doves and bulbuls singing in the hotel garden, they drove on to Tel Aviv. 'I must say Tel Aviv is pretty bleak,' she reported to Celia; 'I was prepared for the worst but it is uglier than my wildest fears.' However, the atmosphere was electric, punctuated by air raids, blackouts and false alarms that initially kept them pinned to their waterfront hotel while Arthur desperately tried to work out what was happening on the ground in the ongoing conflict.

It was Mamaine's first visit to the Middle East, and all was chaos in the newly minted state of Israel – so new that their visas were issued with serial numbers 5 and 6. The Immigration Officer and Customs Inspector had not yet been issued their uniforms, and those who greeted them seemed 'equally affable, inefficient and enthusiastic', in Arthur's report for the *Manchester Guardian*. The Arab leaders had mostly fled, leaving a volatile political vacuum in Haifa, Acre, Jaffa, Tiberias and other cities. Meanwhile, the Palestinian populace did what they could to muddle through, tilling their land, grudgingly selling their produce to their new Jewish overlords, fearful of the situation yet some, at that point, reluctantly receptive to the economic benefits of occupation. 'The road was lively with requisitioned passenger buses wearing primitive mud camouflage and filled

Mamaine with Sabby

with singing Haganah men, trucks with armour plating trying to look like tanks, and similar makeshift contraptions of war.'[27]

Mamaine and Arthur were planning to spend some months in Palestine so that Arthur could report on the war and collect material for a new book, a sequel to *Thieves in the Night,* to be titled *Promise and Fulfilment.* This was to be a more personal, close-up view of the struggle between Israel and Palestine, and – although Arthur did not explicitly envisage it as such – a canvas on which he would tease out his unresolved relationship with his own Jewishness, and with the culture and history of the Jewish state, once and for all. The stakes were high, and the political situation could hardly have been more unsettled on their arrival, stoked by various acts of atrocious violence on both sides and by what was widely seen as the perfidy of the British in abandoning the country to consume itself in civil war.

The view from Mamaine and Arthur's Tel Aviv hotel window, with the smouldering hulk of the *Altalena* visible in the bay

Eager to explore the country, they managed to commandeer a car to drive them through Galilee and up to the Syrian border, visiting their friend Teddy Kolleck's former kibbutz Ein Gev on the shores of Lake Tiberias. There, they swam in the Jordan ('green and glassy, and I saw a wonderful big kingfisher with a brick-red head'), hearing jackals barking in the hills. Every so often a loud explosion would crack through the air, when an animal stepped on one of the mines planted outside the kibbutzim. They arrived back in Tel Aviv to find the blackened, burnt-out hulk of the *Altalena* cargo ship smouldering in the bay opposite their hotel; it had been commandeered by the Jewish Irgun to smuggle in illegal immigrants, dollars and arms, but was targeted by Ben-Gurion's Haganah forces for breaking the truce. To see such internecine carnage sickened them both.

While Arthur was holed up in Tel Aviv, haranguing Menachem Begin, David Ben-Gurion, Kolleck (later to become mayor of Jerusalem) and other warring leaders

Arthur in the jeep that he drove 'like a maniac' up and down the front

of the newly indepen-
dent state, Mamaine
took lessons in
Hebrew, ran endless
errands and tried to
help him as best she
could with research
for his book. They
acquired a puppy
called Sabby and a
battered jeep, which
Arthur drove up and
down the coastal
strip 'like a maniac'.
She found the heat
and overcrowding

A newspaper image of
Mamaine at large in Tel Aviv

oppressive and used the jeep to escape to a quiet spot
by a river outside the city, where she would sit for hours
watching kingfishers, several at a time, playing around
and perching on the rocks under a grove of palm trees.
The temperature rose steadily, the war simmered on
between ragged truces, and in July Mamaine set off to
Jerusalem with a Leica camera (bought on the advice of the
Hungarian-American Robert Capa, also stationed there)
and a brief from Arthur to record all that she saw.

She was relieved to escape, however briefly, from Tel
Aviv, where Arthur's political machinations were getting
him into serious hot water. Tensions between him and
Mamaine were further exacerbated by the attentions of
the *New York Times* stringer Cy Sulzberger, first encountered earlier that year in Trieste, who, without his wife in

attendance, unwisely developed a crush on her. In another of their blazing rows she told Arthur that she could no longer live with him, a decision he accepted with relative equanimity, owning up to a litany of character failings. He was, as Mamaine recognised, always clear-eyed about his own faults, but that was small compensation for having to live with them. She admitted to Celia, 'I realise more than ever that I only feel free and happy when I'm not with K,' and made her decision to return to Wales without him – but not before saving their jeep from five would-be robbers by shouting 'Thieves in the Night!' at them in Hebrew, 'to the great astonishment of Arthur, who was sleeping peacefully when he suddenly heard this flood of invective and woke to see me leaning out of the window and yelling,' as she later recalled in a letter to Edmund.

It was the nearest that Mamaine and Arthur had come to a breaking point, exacerbated by the simmering, endlessly shifting political tensions of the region, Arthur's passionate but not always productive partisanship, the ratcheting rivalries, the crowded days and oppressive heat. For the time being, Mamaine took herself off to Cyprus to cool off – literally and emotionally – by the sea, and regained her equilibrium as she swam and birdwatched and found solace in much-needed solitude before plunging back into a new chapter of her life with Arthur.

CHAPTER 13

COLD WAR

Celia's time in Paris had not been without its setbacks and disappointments, nor had she found her work rewarding enough to absorb her completely. Freddie was now expunged from her heart, and she decided to return home. Her arrival in a still war-blighted London, early in the spring of 1949, coincided with the gathering frostiness in relations between the Soviet Union and the West. Orwell had been the first to describe this situation, unrolling under the overarching nuclear threat, as a 'cold war'. This hostility was articulated more at an official than a popular level, where public opinion was still at least partly sympathetic to Russia after her sufferings as a loyal ally during the war, and because of the equation in many people's minds of communism with progressive policies, peace and disarmament.

In the public sphere, Arthur Koestler and George Orwell had been two of the most prominent voices denouncing the Soviet system for what it was, in their novels *Darkness at Noon* and *Animal Farm* as well as in countless essays and articles. *Nineteen Eighty-Four* was still in gestation and would not be published until June 1949, only six months before the death of its author, who by January that year had been admitted to Cranham Sanatorium, a nursing home in Gloucestershire, where he was to spend much of the year. 'Dearest Celia, How delightful to get your letter and know that you are in England again,' he wrote in mid-February. 'I'm quite comfortable and well looked after,' he reassured her, 'I had really been ill since about September of last year, but I could not go for treatment till the end of the year because I had to finish a book I had been messing about with for a long time' – this, of course, was *Nineteen Eighty-Four*. He promised her a copy 'when it comes out (about June I think), but I don't expect you'll like it; it's an awful book really. I hope you'll stay in England and that I'll see you some time.'

Polemic had folded in 1947, shortly after Celia left for Paris, after eight issues packed with articles and essays by the leading lights of the day, and she now found herself in search of engaging work in London. She was alerted by Koestler to the existence of a faintly mysterious branch of the Foreign Office that was keen to recruit more staff to its mission. The Information Research Department, or IRD, had been created in February 1948 by Ernest Bevin, Foreign Secretary in the Atlee government, as 'a small section in the Foreign Office to collect information about Communist policy, tactics and propaganda and to provide material for our anti-Communist publicity through our missions and information services abroad.'[28] Its aim, essentially, was to put forward a rival ideology to communism, to counter the latter's insidious and many-tentacled spread in the West. Needless to say, Koestler had been among the IRD's early advisors.

Keen to capitalise on the defeat of the Axis powers in 1945, in the 'Great Patriotic War', the Soviet Union was extending its sphere of influence well beyond Eastern Europe, tapping into the goodwill engendered by the key role that Communist parties throughout Europe had played in resisting the Nazis. To that end, Stalin created the Cominform, or Informational Bureau of Communist Parties, in October 1947, to spread the reach of international communism under the guise of peace organisations, trades unions and labour movements. Alarmed by the apparent march of communism on Berlin, Paris and Rome, the British Foreign Office decided to go on the offensive.

The architect of the IRD was Christopher Mayhew, a Labour MP and Foreign Office mandarin who had encountered the blistering power of the Soviet propaganda machine at the United Nations in October 1947, where his boss Ernest Bevin was 'belaboured by Molotov and Vishinsky with a torrent of well-researched information, misinformation, and disinformation, obviously the product of a very large machine for influencing opinion.'[29] What was needed, Mayhew concluded, was a new department under the umbrella of the Foreign Office that could disseminate counter-propaganda in the form of well-researched briefings to the media throughout Europe and Asia, and to the United Nations, a crucially influential forum. The aim was to unite the Free World, even at the price of widening the gap with the Soviet Union and its satellites.

The Foreign Office also had to contend with the 'cosy' reputation of Uncle Joe at home, which the British government had helped create during the war by willingly overlooking the excesses of Stalinism and conniving in the illusion that communism was politically acceptable. 'We had built up this man, although we knew he was terrible, because he was an ally,' explained Adam Watson, second-in-command at the IRD and Celia's future boss.[30] Now the IRD set out to dismantle this mindset in favour of its opposite, an implacable opposition to all that Stalin represented.

Offices were found at Carlton House Terrace, a rabbit-warren of seedy rooms spread over several buildings with one cramped lift. Though there was no heating, the building had copious supplies of hot water, to the delight of underpaid secretaries who could not afford heating at home and would lock themselves in the bathroom to soak happily in the bathtub, among tottering piles of top-secret files, whenever their duties allowed it.

Celia was recruited by Watson, deputy to Ralph Murray, who was charged to run the IRD from its inception. A man of formidable intellect and drive, Murray built a small but dedicated staff involved in intelligence-gathering. Some came from the diplomatic service and others, like Celia, were employed for their language, research and editorial skills, or their backgrounds in other wartime information organisations. Prominent among these was Robert Conquest, a poet, soldier and diplomat, recently returned from Soviet-controlled Bulgaria, where he had witnessed at first hand the violent 'purging' of everyone remotely connected with democracy or Western values. Indeed, he had had to smuggle several Bulgarian friends and colleagues out of the country to save their lives.

At this point, the future author of *The Great Terror* – his 1968 exposé of the Soviet show trials of the 1930s and the horrors of the Gulag – barely spoke any Russian at all, though he could read the language reasonably well; during the eight years he spent at the IRD he would amass a vast knowledge of the Soviet system by piecing together facts from undercover, or *samizdat*, material emanating from the Soviet sphere, and drawing deductions where facts were missing, which they frequently were. 'I felt increasing horror at what was going on, and what had been going on, there. And even greater horror at the success of the Stalinist campaign of falsification, not merely in the Soviet Union, but also in the West, where the voices of truth were commonly ignored or slandered,' Conquest was later to write.[31]

For eighteen months he and Celia shared an office. 'She was one of the nicest, as well as most beautiful, people in the world, and – as did Orwell and many others – I fell for her,' he remembered. A prolific poet, Conquest wrote several love poems to her, 'personal, self-revealing, deeply felt, whatever their virtues otherwise' in his words, which she was touched to receive. One, entitled 'Absence in Mountains', was 'about Celia going to an Alpine sanatorium. I did miss her! There was talk, perhaps later, of her having to live in the Alps for health reasons, and my suggesting – though I'm sure she didn't take it seriously – that in that case I could throw everything else over and do the same [...] I remember speaking of this quite often – perhaps she just let me indulge a fantasy.'[32]

If only the timing had been different Celia might have grown to return Conquest's affection, for she relished his erudite and amusing company and admired his forensic focus and intellectual flair, but her heart was already committed elsewhere: she had recently met the barrister Jeremy

Celia, back from Paris

Hutchinson, and they had fallen deeply and mutually in love. Out of discretion (Jeremy was married) she felt unable to tell Conquest of this development.

One important principle for all the staff at IRD was to establish in advance that the experts they would brief to write for them did not harbour secret communist sympathies. This was far from clear-cut, since the Diplomatic Service was, as is now well known, itself home to certain undercover 'fellow travellers', even outright spies. Celia remembered that she solicited several opinions on articles she had written from Guy Burgess, formerly at the IRD and now on the China Desk, little suspecting his real sympathies. (He had only lasted two months at the IRD in early 1948 before being sacked by Christopher Mayhew for being drunk and degenerate, and had certainly informed his Soviet handlers of everything that he had learned there.) At any rate, the IRD regularly approached journalists, historians and public intellectuals to author articles exposing the lies endemic in the Soviet system at the time, which the department would distribute as widely as possible through their diplomatic channels. It also purchased copies of books that would further their message for wide dissemination: Orwell's *Animal Farm* and Koestler's *Darkness at Noon* were, unsurprisingly, prominent among these.

Knowing well Orwell's views on the Soviet threat, and remembering articles that he had written for *Polemic* which expanded on these views, it is hardly surprising that Celia thought it worth asking George for his advice on IRD's choice of writers and public intellectuals to approach to further its aims. In his essay 'The Prevention of Literature', which appeared in Issue 2 of *Polemic*, in January 1946, Orwell had written:

> The fog of lies and misinformation that surrounds such subjects as the Ukraine famine, the Spanish civil war, Russian policy in Poland, and so forth, is not due entirely to conscious dishonesty, but any writer who is fully sympathetic to the USSR – sympathetic, that is, in the way the Russians themselves would

want him to be – does have to acquiesce in deliberate falsification on important issues.

He continued, in a direct foreshadowing of *Nineteen Eighty-Four*, the novel he was just about to embark upon:

> From the totalitarian point of view history is some-thing to be created rather than learned. A totali-tarian state is effectively a theocracy, and its ruling caste, in order to keep its position, has to be thought of as infallible. But since, in practice, no one is infallible, it is frequently necessary to rearrange past events in order to show that this or that mistake was not made, or that this or that imaginary triumph actually happened. [...] Totalitarianism demands, in fact, the continuous alteration of the past, and in the long run probably demands a disbelief in the very existence of objective truth. The friends of totalitarianism in this country usually tend to argue that since absolute truth is not available, a big lie is no worse than a little lie.

With these views of his in mind, as well as a strong desire to see her old friend again, and with the blessing of her colleagues at the IRD, Celia went to visit George at Cranham on 29 March. She would have gone sooner but his health prevented it; as it was, they had to meet in a horribly damp wooden hut and keep a distance from one another for fear of contagion, while eating a lunch prin-cipally consisting of tinned peas. It must have been a poi-gnant reunion for two friends separated for several years, during which time Orwell's illness had reduced him, physically, to a shadow of his former self. One assumes they talked of many things, of Jura and Paris, of Richard (now in the care of Orwell's sister Avril) and Inez and Arthur and Mamaine, of his writing and her new post in an organisation that chimed so closely with his long-held convictions. Celia recorded in her official memorandum of their meeting to her colleagues at the IRD that Orwell 'expressed his whole-hearted and enthusiastic approval of our aims'. He was too ill, he admitted, to write anything for the IRD himself, and he didn't like writing to commission, though he suggested a few people who might. He followed up in early April with a letter offering, in strictest confidence, to provide his list of those 'who should not be trusted as propagandists', aware that his accusations could be deemed libellous.

Sometime in the mid-to-late-1940s Orwell had started keeping a notebook with names of those he suspected of being still sympathetic to the communist cause or duped by its relentless propaganda. His own clear disillusionment reached back to his experiences in Barcelona during the Spanish Civil War, when he observed at close quarters the ruthless treachery of, and the betrayal of colleagues by, Spanish Communists who were ostensibly their allies. He strongly suspected British pro-Soviet sympathies to be behind his difficulties in getting *Animal Farm* published in 1945. He watched the relentless advance of Russian Communism via the 1948 coup d'état in Czechoslovakia and the ten-month Soviet blockade of West Berlin, which was only to be lifted on 12 May 1949. In his enfeebled state he could not do much but try to offer assistance to the only organisation currently focused on countering this gathering threat.

On 2 May he duly sent Celia the promised 'list with about 35 names.' (There were, in fact, thirty-eight.) He qualified:

> It isn't very sensational and I don't suppose it will tell your friends anything they don't know. At the same time it isn't a bad idea to have the people who are probably unreliable listed. If it had been done earlier it would have stopped people like Peter Smollett worming their way into important propaganda jobs where they were probably able to do us a lot of harm. Even as it stands I imagine this list is very libellous, or slanderous, or whatever the term is, so will you please see that it is returned to me without fail [...]

The list was typed up and filed in the IRD on 4 May 1949, and didn't see the light of day until I found a typewritten copy of it in a file after my mother's death in 2002. There had been fevered speculation as to who might be on it when, in July 1996, the fact of its existence emerged through documents released under the Public Record Office's thirty-year rule. The question is, why did Celia not reveal it at the time and put the record straight then, or while she was alive? She couldn't: the list was classified, and the original only released by the Foreign Office soon after the article that I commissioned from Timothy Garton Ash, setting the list in its proper context, was published in the *Guardian Saturday Review* in June 2003.[33]

In 1996, Celia had attempted to quell the controversy surrounding it and the catcalls from voices on the Left accusing Orwell of betraying his friends, by stating adamantly – and correctly – that those named in the list were not his friends. 'I think George was quite right to do it,' she insisted. 'And, of course, everybody thinks that people were going to be shot at dawn. The only thing that was going to happen to them was that they wouldn't be asked to write for the Information Research Department.'

It was arguably a storm in a teacup, but – as Garton Ash reminds us – it showed up the double standards in play at the time. Had the list been of crypto-Nazis, or of 'people who would go over to the Nazi side if Germany won the war' as Orwell posited in a 'London Letter' column in *Partisan Review* in 1942, there would probably have been no fuss at all.

As it was, Orwell's accusations were mild, often amounting to no more than a single or double question mark beside certain names: Charlie Chaplin, J. B. Priestley, Michael Redgrave. The scurrilous MP and journalist Tom Driberg earned a reprieve: 'Usually named as "crypto" but in my opinion NOT reliably pro C.P.' The historian E. H. Carr was labelled 'Appeaser only' while Kingsley Martin, editor of the *New Statesman*, earned the comment '??Too dishonest to be outright "crypto" or fellow-traveller, but reliably pro-Russian on all major issues.' Orwell's worst barb was aimed at Peter Smollett (born Smolka in Vienna, like a character out of a John le Carré novel) who 'gives the strong impression of being some kind of Russian agent. Very slimy person.' Formerly head of the Russian section of the Ministry of Information during the war, Smollett was after his death outed as a Soviet agent recruited by Kim Philby, and is thought to have been the 'important official in the Ministry of Information' who persuaded Jonathan Cape not to publish *Animal Farm* in 1944. These individuals, and others whose names are now largely drowned out by the passing of the years, were indeed not commissioned to write for the IRD. Otherwise, their lives continued uninterrupted by the long arm of the state; some even received honours (Smollett got the OBE).

Back in 1949, Celia visited George again in May, and sent him a welcome bottle of brandy, and Orwell picked up the correspondence in June to commiserate with her about her latest illness, necessitating a bronchoscopy – 'I hope you are taking care of yourself and getting strong.' He had received a bottle of brandy from Mamaine, too, for his forty-sixth birthday, and a surprise visit from Sonia Brownell, a friend of both twins from *Horizon* days and the woman towards whom Orwell now redirected his romantic interest. In early September he moved from Cranham to University College Hospital in Gower Street, and thereafter Celia was able to visit him more regularly, 'But I didn't see as much of him as I would have liked,' she remembered with regret.

She was pleased, if sceptical, about Orwell's proposed marriage to Sonia. She was a perceptive judge of character and recognised, beneath Sonia's diamond-bright manner, a deep and unassuageable unhappiness. As she recalled:

> We all knew Sonia very well. She was a lovely person, and she was unbelievably generous. Also she was rather lovely looking. She had enormous

shining blue eyes, fair hair, a rather voluptuous, luscious-looking woman, but the kind of life she led didn't quite go with the kind of person she looked as though she was. She elected to lead an intellectual's life, when she wasn't really an intellectual, although she loved literature. She was a person of feeling, that's what she really was, and I should imagine that's what George saw in her, someone with a warm heart. She was a very unhappy person, always. She was basically unbelievably unhappy. She kept up always a smiling facade with her friends because she wanted her friends to have a good time.[34]

Many, including Sonia herself, seemed perplexed by the marriage; she had after all turned George down when he first proposed to her in 1945, and now she confessed to Celia, 'It's rather sad to marry an old, sick man,' perhaps forgetting that Orwell was only forty-six. There was no pretence of real romance from either George or Sonia. But Arthur Koestler was delighted by the news that his friend was to marry again; if Celia had foiled his wish that she should marry George, then Sonia, in his view, was a worthy alternative. He wrote from France to congratulate Orwell:

I have been saying for years that she is the nicest, most intelligent and decent girl that I met during my whole stay in England. She is precisely for that reason also very lonely in that crowd in which she moves and she will become a changed person when you take her out of it. I think I had a closer view of the Connolly set-up than you did; it has a steady

Alfresco at Ritz Representatives
after the wedding of:
George Orwell & Sonia   Mary Brownell
Eric Blair

MENU   Robert Kee

Huitres

Filets de Sole d'Antin

Supreme de Volaille à la Ritz

Haricots Verts

Pommes Noisette

Poire Melba

Celia Kirwan

Sonia Blair

Café

13th October 1949.

The menu for the Orwells' wedding lunch at the Ritz

stultifying effect which had an effect even on a tough guy like me.

He ends by hoping – unrealistically – that he and Mamaine will at some point have a chance to 'see you both again and pop champagne corks into the Seine.'[35]

Both Celia and Mamaine attended the wedding lunch that David Astor threw for the Orwells' marriage on 13 October at the Ritz, though George himself was far too ill to attend (the legal marriage had taken place earlier that day in his hospital room at UCL). All the lunch guests – Robert and Janetta Kee, James McGibbon (Kee's publishing partner), Roger Senhouse (of Orwell's publisher Secker & Warburg), along with the twins, Sonia and David Astor – signed the menu card, which detailed Oysters, Suprême de Volaille à la Ritz and Poire Melba, inter alia, and, thanks to Astor's generosity and Sonia's propensity for a party, they contrived to make it as gay an occasion as they could. Thereafter, some friends thought George looked brighter on their visits to him, but the overall trajectory was down, as he visibly wasted away in his hospital bed.

Celia visited him when she could, observing his decline with a sinking heart. She was sharp about Sonia to Mamaine after a visit in early January 1950: 'Sonia is worried whether she will have enough money to write, or enough time from looking after G. Of course that is just making excuses to avoid having to start. I still think that if she'd been a <u>really</u> determined character she could have written every morning for a couple of hours and perhaps had fewer late nights.' On 20 January 1950, as Celia recalled, 'I rang him up and said, "When can I come and see you, George?" And he said, "Well I'm going off next Wednesday with Sonia to Switzerland." And I said, "Oh that's wonderful news, George, they must think you are going to get better." And he said, "Either that, or they don't want a corpse on their hands." Well, then he said, "Come next Monday" and the next morning a friend of Cyril Connolly rang me up to say that George had died the night before, the very night of the day I'd rung him up.' An artery had burst in his lungs, and the resulting haemorrhage killed him.

Her sadness can be imagined. She had loved him, if not as a potential husband, then as a friend of the utmost constancy. There was a faint relief that the suffering of his last months was over, that the long-anticipated finale had come, but nevertheless an overwhelming sense of loss engulfed her. His had been a poignant presence, and absence, ever since their first meeting in 1945, and both were keenly aware of one another's longings and vulnerabilities.

Writing to Edmund Wilson that autumn about the death of their mutual friend, Mamaine told him, 'It is extraordinary how much everyone who knew him well misses George Orwell; his friends talk about him all the time, there is a real void since he died.' Koestler summed him up as a man whose intellectual honesty 'made him appear almost inhuman at times' but also made him 'the only writer of genius among the *littérateurs* of social revolt between the two wars'.[36]

Celia often talked about George through the years – with Inez, Arthur and Sonia of course, who had their own memories, and with us, her children, as we were growing up. She remembered him with deep affection and a certain ruefulness – what if they had married, after all, albeit for the brief autumn of his life? She spent her mid-thirties, instead, in a tumultuous affair of the heart before settling down in 1954 with our father, Arthur Goodman, another man of deeply serious intent. She never truly regretted her decision, only that she had not felt able to give George the happiness he desired, when he desired it, and before it was too late.

CHAPTER 14

VERTE RIVE

Returning much restored from Cyprus in autumn 1948, Mamaine concluded that the crisis in her relationship with Arthur, exacerbated by the strains of Israel, was no longer terminal. As it happened, a new episode in their lives was about to unfold, this time in France. A childhood friend of Arthur's, the Hungarian Paul Winkler,

Verte Rive at Fontaine le Port

prosperous, expansive and a great admirer of Arthur's writings, now offered the couple his sixteenth-century chateau at Chartrettes, on the banks of the Seine opposite the Forêt de Fontainebleau, in order for Arthur to write his book on Palestine. There they hunkered down in late autumn, working flat out in an effort to finish *Promise and Fulfilment* by mid-January 1949. Mamaine reported to Celia that in the lead-up to Christmas they both worked between eleven and twelve hours a day, starting at nine and often finishing after midnight, sometimes at 2 a.m.

It was an exhausting routine, and Mamaine made a 'strike notice' to pin above Arthur's desk with large letters in pink and white urging MORE CARROTS LESS STICK, to no avail. The work went on, but they achieved a new harmony in their mutual focus and absorption, and by dint of steering Arthur away from his more partisan observations Mamaine reported that the book was shaping up well as a fairly impartial 'outsider's' view on the complex situation in Palestine.

Despite the pressure, they managed to escape into the Fontainebleau forest for occasional walks, which were pure joy for Mamaine, with her ear always cocked for birds: the forest and riverbank were alive with nightingales, nightjars, various warblers, chiffchaffs and redstarts. They liked the area so much that they started looking for a house of their own. The damp of riverside living might not be good for her lungs, she knew; nevertheless, the search was underway. They

had now turned their backs definitively on Wales, Paris was within an hour's drive for injections of social life, and they soon found a pretty house called Verte Rive at Fontaine-le-Port which seemed an answer to all their dreams. Built on the river's bank, it had steps down to a jetty on the Seine, from where they could swim and scull about in a dinghy, which Arthur loved to do.

Needless to say, the house turned out to be far from perfect on closer acquaintance, but they had bought it by then and resolved to make the most of it. The damp river air in winter, however, was a threat to Mamaine's health, as she had suspected it would be, and she was soon seriously unwell. She found an asthma specialist in Paris, whom Celia had consulted the year before, and implored Celia to send her a detailed medical history, with details of all the drugs that she had tried and their results. 'What was the one that nearly made you croak?' she wondered. As it happened, it was Novocaine, which had given Celia a nearly fatal allergic reaction in a hospital in England, but Celia was not able to get the message to Mamaine in time, and a couple of days later Mamaine herself was injected with Novocaine, with disastrous results. She was temporarily paralysed and nearly died; certain that her life was fading while lucid as day, she longed to tell Arthur she loved him before she died, but was unable to speak. 'The frustration of having one's dying words all ready, and not being able to say them!' she wrote later to Celia. She couldn't resist a rebuke, though the postal system was the real culprit: 'I can't get over how nearly you were responsible for my death by not warning me about Novocaine: it really is carrying irresponsibility a bit far.'

Characteristically, though, she made light of her collapse, which was keeping her in bed for weeks, while Arthur struggled with arranging the furniture and rugs, newly arrived from Wales. 'It is lovely to be able to lie in bed and look out on the river with its barges and tugs gliding past. It is a very sunny house, too [...] Oh the river is so lovely, I wish you could see it, it's so quiet and the chaffinches sing away in the forest opposite, herons rise up out of the reeds and motor barges chug along making a pleasant noise and leaving a trail behind them of glassy water . . .' She ends her letter by sympathising with Celia's current emotional dilemma occasioned by Robert Conquest's persistent attentions: 'I am sorry for you – it is a dog's life having people wanting to marry one, unkind as it sounds to say so.'

Her illness dragged on through the spring, serious enough to force a lengthy admission to hospital in Paris in April '49, which shocked Arthur into feverish action, chivvying doctors and chasing prescriptions and caring for her as best he could. Despite the physical suffering, she was able to report to Celia during her convalescence in May:

Since my illness K and I have sometimes been able to talk to each other in a new, much deeper way, saying things one can't usually say to anybody at all & with a wonderful understanding between us. [...] I am still reading *Anna Karenina*, rationing it to a few pages a day, & it seems to me it is one of the greatest joys one can have, to re-read these Tolstoy novels. I do wish you hadn't done so recently, & that you had the time to do it at the same time as

Hard at work on *Promise and Fulfilment*

me, so that we could discuss them as we went along.
I am simply obsessed by them.

Camus had tried to visit her in hospital, missing her by a whisker, and news of his attempt reminded her of how the last time she saw him she was struck 'by his expression, at the same time serious, tender and resolute – for all his faults he is the best of men'. Celia had recently visited George Orwell in his sanatorium at Cranham and told Mamaine how terribly ill he looked: 'I <u>am</u> sorry about Donkey George – how very sad,' she commiserated.

During Mamaine's agonisingly slow recovery, she charted the spring arrival of birds in the forest in her letters to Celia, and the sisters swapped notes on books they were both reading, from Simone Weil's *Waiting for God* to T. S. Eliot's *The Cocktail Party*. An easier pace of life resumed over the summer, as Arthur was now engaged on a novel, which didn't involve Mamaine in the type of research that his non-fiction books demanded. Nevertheless, she was tormented by anxiety after the trauma of her brush with death, and losing weight so fast that Arthur flew her over to a nursing home in Hampstead, where she could rest and fatten up before being given a bronchoscopy. From feeling like 'a gibbering maniac' on admission, she gradually regained some peace of mind, writing reflectively to Arthur:

> Darling,
>
> Better than ever today, and what's more, my psychotherapy has worked so my troubles are over. I was so excited, at night, to find I could suddenly <u>think</u> again about the things I do usually think about, that I could hardly sleep [...]
>
> It is a relief to feel, as I do, that my mind is normal again. But you know, since my illness all my ideas about every serious problem, from politics – if that is a serious problem – to ethics, the life of the spirit or whatever you like to call it, & all the rest, are in a state of great confusion. [...] I am <u>not</u> the victim of a diseased mind when I say that my attitude to God seems to be thoroughly unsatisfactory – though I give that one up for the time being. I feel that I have been taking for granted certain things, ways of looking at things, or systems, which I had either worked out for myself or got from you, & that one can't really take anything for granted for long without being guilty of the sin of intellectual arrogance.

If I <u>do</u> hit on any striking conclusions, they will be embodied in my book on my illness, to be entitled

TURNIP'S TESTAMENT
Or
DIALOGUE WITH LIFE
No more for the moment. . . . love, M

Recovered, rested and somewhat refreshed, she returned to Verte Rive, where life picked up speed again. They had polyglot friends to visit from all over Europe, and daily swimming and canoeing on the river. There were regular escapades to Paris to dine with various luminaries, though no longer with Sartre and de Beauvoir who had taken the

Sculling about in boats, one of Arthur's favourite occupations

position that 'someone who is a friend of Malraux can't be a friend of theirs – can you beat it?' as Mamaine exclaimed to Celia. *Je n'y comprends plus rien,*' she continued, 'except that all French intellectuals are raving mad.' The problem was deeper than that: Koestler deplored Sartre's equivocation about the Soviet Union, the way he diminished the endemic evils of the Soviet Gulag camps by comparing them with temporary detention camps in Europe, thereby cauterising their horror. The irony was that Arthur and Mamaine never saw Malraux now, either.

But post-war Paris was a lively bouillabaisse of writers and artists from Europe and the States – Raymond Aron, Stephen Spender and James Burnham among them – many of whom lionised Arthur and were charmed by Mamaine, so the invitations flowed in. Their social life, however, was a minefield, thanks to the fact that Arthur, with almost supernatural powers, could scent a former communist or communist sympathiser at a mile, and now loathed the Gaullists every bit as much, having lost all faith in their integrity, too. Mamaine's nerves were often shredded as a result.

At one of these dinners they were encouraged to bring in their dog Sabby who immediately attacked the resident Alsatian: 'a terrible fight ensued, everybody fell very ineffectively on the dogs to try and separate them, and soon K, the only effective one, was lying on the ground hanging onto Sabby's collar while somebody else was holding Sabby's legs in the air, & I was trying to disengage the Alsatian's jaws from Sabby's ear and Sabby's jaws from the Alsatian's throat . . .' At least this was a distraction from the relentlessly highbrow conversation which typically

Mamaine and Arthur, shortly before their marriage

dragged on long into the night while everyone drank too much and became argumentative, Arthur chief among them. One particular blinder ended in Arthur, dead drunk, punching a policeman who discovered him asleep in his car and being taken into the cells where he was roughed up before being dispatched home to await trial – to Mamaine's secret delight, as she could see no other way of curtailing his drinking than giving him a good fright. His contrition was profound, but alas short-lived.

This much was proved on the night of their wedding on 15 April 1950. They had had to wait to formalise their union until Arthur's divorce papers from his brief first marriage to Dorothy Ascher in 1935 had come through, and neither made much of the event, given that they had been married in all but name for six years. Mamaine even discouraged Celia from making the trip over to Paris for the ceremony. But she must have hoped that marriage to Arthur would consolidate and calm their rocky relationship, for she had continued to believe in him, and love him, through thick and thin. She wrote to Celia just days before the wedding, summing up her position:

In fact I am awfully happy with K simply because I do love him so much, not a day goes by without my thinking what happiness it is for me to be with him.[...] Whatever happens to me from now on – and I have no reason to think that anything awful will – I shall consider my life has been well spent since I have spent six years of it with K. For apart from anything else I greatly believe in K as a writer, and I would do anything, even leave him if it were

Married in Paris

Wedding⸱ in Paris is made known to-day of Arthur Koest- ler, Hungarian-born writèr, and Mamaine Paget (pictured here), one of the much-photo- graphed "Paget twins." Miss Paget, 33, is daughter of the late Mr. and Mrs. Eric M. Pag⸱t.

necessary, to help him fulfil what I consider to be his destiny. I should count myself and my life of little importance in such a case.

They were married in the morning at the British Consulate with a couple of friends as witnesses, fol- lowed by a convivial and delicious lunch at the Cochon d'Or, and that, had Mamaine had her way, would have been that. However, that was never that with Arthur: he was spoiling for a night on the tiles. So they met up with Stephen Spender and various friends at the Café Flore that evening, and progressed from there to dinner, and then to a nightclub, Arthur getting increasingly drunk, maudlin and emotional along the way. When Mamaine refused to let him drive her home in view of his extreme inebriation, he slammed the car door and drove off into the darkness, leaving her to spend the night chastely in Spender's flat on the Boulevard St Germain. Over breakfast the follow- ing day, Spender commented ruefully, 'I've always wanted to spend the night with you, Mamaine; just too bad it had to be your wedding night,' before accompanying her to the Orangerie to an exhibition of German Primitives. Arthur meanwhile was racked with guilt and self-loathing, claiming that, were there such a thing as a non-religious monastery, he should check himself in to achieve the mortification of the flesh and the real life of the spirit, and vowing for the umpteenth time to completely give up drink – except for weekends, that invaluable get-out clause.

During their sojourn in France, Arthur had become involved with planning and drafting the manifesto for the founding conference of the Congress for Cultural Freedom, to be held in the ruins of post-Hitler Berlin in late June 1950. It was the culmination of a series of propaganda shoot-outs between the Soviet Union and the West – in which the Soviets had been, hitherto, the undoubted winners – under the guise of glittering international peace conferences. Dissenting voices had always been excluded, or neutered or forced into uttering mere 'banalities and empty rhetoric' in the case of poor Dmitri Shostakovich, who had been forced to take the stand at the riotous Waldorf conference in New York in March 1949. Orwell, Russell, Malraux, Camus and Koestler were not alone in agitating for some urgent initiative in order to save the free world, and Arthur, with his energy and passion, was petitioned in 1949 to help make this a reality. No cause could have been closer to his heart.

He had constantly advocated in articles and essays ('Memoirs of a Tightrope Walker' for Richard Crossman's collection *The God That Failed* among them) a cultural counter-offensive against the continuing expansion of

Soviet control and manipulation: this was his chance to turn his ideas to practical effect. At moments of emergency such as this – and the first day of the conference was dominated by the news that North Korea had invaded the South – it was idiotic to 'preach neutrality towards the bubonic plague,' as he put it. Koestler's impassioned speeches, and his fourteen-point 'Freedom Manifesto', proudly declaimed to a crowd of fifteen thousand on the last day of the conference, made him the hero of the hour. 'We hold it to be self-evident that intellectual freedom is one of the inalienable rights of man,' he declared, and wound up in German with the rallying cry, 'Friends, freedom has seized the Offensive!' Reading his Manifesto today it is extraordinary how prescient and relevant it still is, more than seventy years on, as we survey the graveyards of individual freedoms in Russia, North Korea, China and Hong Kong, Iran, Afghanistan and much of the Middle East, and the ongoing threats to democracy and freedom of speech and action in the West.

Koestler was in his element in Berlin: at last he had a challenge of existential proportions that called on his skills and deepest convictions, and he rose charismatically to the occasion. Mamaine had been more sceptical, however, writing to Edmund

Mamaine and Arthur arriving at the Berlin Conference for Cultural Freedom, from *Der Tag*

Wilson, 'K is going to Berlin at the end of this month, for what is sure to be a mucked-up conference of mushheads, as these things always are.' He and Mamaine travelled by train to Berlin, and, between the feverish preparations for each session and speech, the draftings and redraftings of his Freedom Manifesto (which took on some of the principles of his and Orwell's proposed League for the Rights and Dignity of Man of 1946), they visited as many quarters of the shattered city as they could, talking to Berliners from every walk of life. 'The Berliners are very impressive,' wrote Mamaine, again to Edmund. 'They also have an extraordinary courage and vitality.'

It was a frenetic week, exhausting for both of them, but Arthur was on a roll, cajoling, persuading, explaining, declaiming, and deftly maintaining the peace between dissenting factions. There were more than a hundred delegates at the Congress from all over the world, comprising a who's-who of public intellectuals of the liberal left and not-so-left. Some, like Arthur and Stephen Spender, were former communists who had seen the light, others at the conservative end of the spectrum, but, whatever their differences, most were swept up in Arthur's eloquent and impassioned call to arms on the final day.

Among the delegates from Britain were Spender, Herbert Read, Hugh Trevor-Roper and Freddie Ayer; other prominent delegates included Melvin Lasky (later to become the editor of *Encounter*), Carlo Levi, Tennessee Williams, Ignazio Silone, Benedetto Croce and the Rabelaisian Nicolas Nabokov, cousin of Vladimir and Secretary-General of the Congress. Spender joined Arthur Koestler and five others on the newly elected executive

Arthur at the helm of the conference

committee to take the initiative forward, and management
of the Secretariat was entrusted to Michael Josselson, who
would later be uncovered as a CIA agent. The covert role
played by Washington and the CIA in establishing and
funding the CCF and its activities – which would range
from publishing magazines the world over, disseminating
books including *Darkness at Noon* to the other side of the
Iron Curtain, promoting exhibitions, prizes and concerts,
and organising high-profile international conferences –
was not fully exposed until 1967, by which time it was
operating in thirty-five countries throughout the world.

Encounter, founded in 1953 by Stephen Spender and
the American political essayist Irving Kristol, and edited
from 1958 by Melvin Lasky, was the chief recipient of
CCF support in Great Britain, and gained a wide reader-
ship among the intelligentsia, few of whom suspected the
ultimate source of its funding. The revelation in 1967 that

Encounter had effectively been a cultural arm of the CIA was more than bruising: as George Weidenfeld remembered, 'So violent was the condemnation of Laski [sic] and his band of "cold warriors" that it spilled over into many different spheres of intellectual life. The battle was waged at the dinner tables in New York's Village and Riverside Drive, London's Hampstead and the high tables of Oxford and Cambridge. It assumed Homeric proportions.'[37]

Spender promptly resigned as literary editor, joining with his wife Natasha in the backlash against Lasky and Josselson, but, nevertheless, the range and distinction of *Encounter's* journalism – and its contributors – kept it in business until 1991 and the end of the Cold War. On its dissolution, Bernard Levin saluted the achievements of its veterans, those Cold Warriors such as Robert Conquest who had stuck with it through the decades, 'the motley army which, without a shot fired, fought for the truth against lies, for reality against mirages, for steadfastness against capitulation, for civilisation against barbarism [...] for, put most simply, democracy against tyranny.'[38] Interestingly, Conquest's *The Great Terror* was revealed by the KGB's own statistics to have underestimated, if anything, the number of victims of Stalinism.

Was Arthur aware of the CIA's involvement in 1950, given his leading role at the conference, both in front of and behind the scenes? Spender was plainly naive in his wilful ignorance of it; Lasky undoubtedly knew the truth and didn't care, such was his commitment to the cause; and Nicolas Nabokov managed to evade the issue entirely, bluffing with enough charm and good humour to put inquisitors off the scent. But what of Arthur? His biographer Michael Scammell claims he had no inkling at the time, but if so, he too would have been blinkered by his dedication to the cause, since the budget and extravagance alone must have indicated substantial backing from a powerful sponsor. Scammell suggests that Koestler assumed this to be the State Department or the Marshall Fund, neither of which made any bones about their hostility to the Soviet Union.[39]

Back in France, Arthur threw himself with fervour into the task of realising the Conference's aims in concrete ways, with newsletters, campaigns and plans for broadcast dialogues with the East. Verte Rive became once again a hive of activity and Arthur obsessed, hardly sleeping at night and keeping Mamaine up till the small hours with his 'ravings' on the subject. He drove himself on relentlessly – when did he ever do anything by halves? – and, by mid-August, was so exhausted that he had a total meltdown and crashed his car, prelude to a rude awakening to the fact that he could not single-handedly steer the CCF forward but must stand back from the fray. Scammell suggests that Arthur's breakdown may have been exacerbated by his dawning realisation of CIA involvement. At any rate, he was summarily removed from the executive committee and agreed to take a well-earned holiday, and to consider a complete move – to America or even to England, at last, to Mamaine's unmitigated joy.

CHAPTER 15

NEW BEGINNINGS

Arthur was nothing if not decisive, and wasted no time in putting any decision into action. He and Mamaine abandoned Verte Rive for London in September 1950. Arthur flew on to the States to explore the possibility of making a more permanent home there, for he felt that he needed a wider view of world affairs which could only be acquired by a deeper immersion in American culture. Mamaine, not sure how this plan would work out, moved in with Celia in Chelsea in the interim, and found herself happier than she had been for quite a while. She was no longer living on a knife-edge, unsure every day which way the wind would blow. The twins took up piano lessons with Joe Cooper (who would present the BBC series 'Face the Music' in the 1970s), both practising for hours every day, and Mamaine reconnected happily with old friends who had not forgotten her. The anxiety that had plagued her since her illness of 1949 evaporated, and she felt rejuvenated. As she confided to Edmund, now her chief correspondent: 'It is so nice living in London; I thought I was an inveterate London-hater but I find I love it really; and partly because it is not too beautiful. Events here have whatever

significance they have, & no more. In Paris, always so shat-
teringly beautiful, everything has a heightened significance
and in the end it becomes intolerable.'

She found Celia absorbed in the throes of her love affair
with the barrister Jeremy Hutchinson, which brought her
joy and anguish in equal measure. Jeremy had been married for some time to the celebrated actress Peggy Ashcroft,
yet by this point felt desperately lonely within his marriage.
Peggy, already at the height of her career (she was eight
years older than Jeremy), was at the theatre every evening
and most weekends and Jeremy had a punishing schedule
at the Bar throughout the week, building a practice that
was to take him to the peak of his profession as QC for the
defence in some of the most celebrated trials of the century.
He and Peggy remained deeply fond of one another but
had simply grown apart, since they barely crossed paths
from week to week.

Jeremy was deliberately introduced to Celia by his
mother, the acute and formidable Mary Hutchinson,
former longtime mistress of Clive Bell, who recognised
Jeremy's loneliness and calculated that Celia might be
the ideal person to assuage it. She arranged a dinner to
introduce them and took Celia to the public gallery for
one of Jeremy's trials, guessing she would be impressed
by his quicksilver wit and devastating cross-examination
in court.

Mary was, as ever, perceptive: the introduction led
to them falling swiftly and deeply in love; for Celia, it
was transformative. For all her admirers and numerous
proposals of marriage, my mother had not let herself be
drawn into a relationship with anyone since her affair in

Jeremy Hutchinson and Celia

1946 with Freddie Ayer, but with Jeremy at last it was
the real thing. However, neither of them could or would
countenance the idea of Jeremy's family falling apart while
his two children, Eliza and Nick, were barely teenagers.
Jeremy's marriage was a fairly open one, so not too much
subterfuge was required, yet there could be no prospect of
making a life together while he was still committed to his
young family. Nevertheless, Celia and Jeremy snatched
what happiness they could, when they could, and their
mutual love and desire filled Celia's life with new meaning.
She found herself as much on the same wavelength with
Jeremy as she felt with Mamaine, and they both recognised
how rare and miraculous their newfound empathy was.
He took her to the tiny island he had bought amid the
mudflats off the coast of Essex, a wilderness of seabirds
and grasses reachable only by dinghy if the tides were too
high for the muddy causeway. There he would go, often
with his children, to 'mess about in boats', or to escape the
pressures of his work and strained marriage. As his son
Nick later described, they would 'paddle across to the old
hulk of a houseboat beached on the mud.'

This was the quintessential place to mess about in boats, watched over by the spirit of Arthur Ransom who used the island as a location in his sailing stories. There was the dinghy whose main purpose was to get us out to *Secret Waters*, a beautiful Brightlingsea half-decked roller jib, the perfect day sailor. Then the much-used 'duck punt', almost canoe-like, which could explore all the hidden waterways, light and manoeuvrable, my favourite. On land, one little hut a short distance from the houseboat, with just a few tools (Jeremy was no handyman). The rest of the island was flat and almost treeless except for the famous Heronry with at least a dozen trees.[40]

The island is still uninhabited and inaccessible; now a nature reserve, its soundtrack still the whistle of the wind, the cries of waders and the rise and fall of the tides.

Jeremy would also take Celia down to Chichester harbour where he was planning to rebuild a tiny boathouse along the strand, a favourite bolthole ever since the wild summer childhood holidays he and his sister Barbara had spent in West Wittering while their parents St John and Mary Hutchinson went about their sophisticated, cultured city lives. In London, Celia and Jeremy snatched moments together whenever they could, around the demands of his family and their working lives, for Celia was soon busily employed on the new magazine *History Today*, founded by her old friend Peter Quennell with Alan Hodge. Theirs was, *force majeure*, a contingent relationship, bounded on all sides, and that both added to its intensity and overlaid its joys with shadow.

Island Farm

At the end of 1950, Mamaine left London again and joined Arthur in the States, where they soon moved into Island Farm, a white weatherboarded house on an island in the Delaware River in Pennsylvania. It was another damp and difficult place to run, with a dearth of domestic help and few close neighbours. But the location made it easy for Mamaine to reconnect with her old American friends, Edmund and Elena Wilson among them, and Eleanor Perényi, by now long separated from her Hungarian husband Zsiga and busy working as a journalist in New York. They met many new ones, 'for we live in Bucks County, the Hecate County of Edmund [Wilson]'s *Memoirs of Hecate County* – full of intellectuals and smarties and show people and everything else', she reported.

Few of these new acquaintances cut much ice, however, nor did the current social and political situation, which they found shallow and cynical, prompting Arthur to ask 'is all this crime and corruption a phenomenon of

In a stately Cadillac; Arthur loved American cars

adolescence or of decay? Police corruption is on a scale unimaginable even to people (like us) who've lived in France.' Arthur was again acclaimed by the US establishment, and they were invited to Boston and Baltimore, Philadelphia and New York, to be wined and dined by various bigwigs and writers. Some they greatly liked, others were not to their taste, notably the 'really awful' Senator McCarthy, 'a hairy-pawed thug of about 40–46' with whom they inadvertently found themselves having drinks on a trip to Washington, DC.

Winter took for ever to turn to spring, and in late March as the rain thundered down Mamaine concluded it never would – 'I don't believe there ever is a spring here, I think it must go straight from winter to summer.' She developed bronchitis and possible pleurisy, exacerbated of course by living on an island, prompting Celia to exclaim: 'About your health . . . you are obviously suffering from too much damp, and just because you happen to be married to a maniac who will insist on choosing the dampest places in the world to live in, it is no reason why you should quietly die off.'

By April, Mamaine was writing to Celia, 'I am happy to say that Arthur is getting absolutely fed up with being in America and is pining to come to Europe [...] this all sounds extremely promising and I am all agog to see what

Arthur with his newly acquired puppy

we will do.' She found herself 'more and more homesick
for Europe. I remember standing in the cloisters of St
Tromphime in Arles and thinking I couldn't bear to live
in a country where nothing like this exists.'

Arthur and Mamaine did indeed return to Europe in
July 1951 – they needed to sell Verte Rive, prior to settling
in England at long last. On a brief trip to Paris, Mamaine
found herself having dinner alone with Camus, Francine
having just left for the country. She hadn't expected to see
him on his own, and believed she couldn't possibly get on
with him if she did, given their history, but after an initial awkwardness their defences broke down. He told her
that he still dreamed of her often, recalling vivid incidents
from their time in Provence together which he thought
he'd forgotten, and that he always felt he could confide
in her completely, so certain was he of her understanding.
'C very tender, his voice, his laugh, his eyes,' she noted in
her diary. 'In the *bal musette* it seemed that we were back

The early draft of 'Retour à Tipasa' that Camus gave to
Mamaine (With permission, © All Rights Reserved.)

in one of the many bars or nightclubs that we've been in together, time standing still around us as it did then, nobody else there but us & the other people simply part of the decor, C looking at me all the time with his tender serious smiling eyes.'

It was shortly after this that Camus gave Mamaine the handwritten manuscript draft of his famous essay 'Retour à Tipasa', one of the four reflections that he would publish in the collection *L'Eté* in 1954. In it, he describes returning to the Roman ruins, sunlight and glittering sea of his native Algeria, remembered through decades of exile. 'When one has had the good luck to love intensely, life is spent trying to recapture that ardour and that illumination. Forsaking beauty and the sensual happiness attached to it, exclusively serving misfortune, calls for a nobility I lack.'[41] He writes of the weight of 'exile, of desiccated life, of dead souls', and of how 'To come alive again one needs a special grace, self-forgetfulness, or a homeland.' At Tipasa, 'under the glorious December light [...] I found exactly what I had come seeking, what, despite the era and the world, was offered me, truly to me alone, in that forsaken nature.' In that light and that silence 'years of wrath and night melted slowly away. I listened to an almost forgotten sound within myself as if my heart, long stopped, were calmly beginning to beat again.' He concludes, 'In the middle of winter I learned at last that there was in me an invincible summer.'[42] In these words of exaltation lay Camus's philosophy of redemption, shared with Mamaine in this early draft, with its bewildering labyrinth of additions, subtractions and rephrasings. The manuscript lay among his letters in my mother's tin trunk, a record of his thoughts and counter-thoughts, of a mind working painfully towards the clarity that gave his best writings their universal reach and moral significance.

Their brief encounter (and reminder of what could have been) would have made Arthur's churlishness on their return to London even more galling than usual. Added to this was the fact that he was half-heartedly sleeping with his devoted secretary Cynthia, whom Mamaine was fond of and had welcomed warmly into their lives. 'Things very bad with K, rows every night at dinner,' she recorded, 'the other day so lost my nerve that I threw glass of Pernod at K across the table. This very unlike me & is a sign that I'm completely worn down.'

A few weeks later, in September 1951, she and Arthur separated for good: only a little more than a year after making it official, their marriage was over. It was Mamaine's decision: utterly exhausted, she could take no more of living with Arthur's argumentativeness, his drinking, his unpredictability, his self-hatred, guilt and wild mood swings, which he always took out on her. After seven years, all of them purposeful, many of them happy and none of them dull, their separation was a cause of deep pain for both, but she felt impelled to rescue herself from emotional burnout. She found herself a small house in South Kensington and Arthur bought another within walking distance, in Montpelier Square. They continued to meet at least once a week and remained affectionately close, but, from then on, they resigned themselves to leading separate lives.

·

Mamaine confessed to Edmund Wilson that, much to her surprise, 'Living alone has a lot to be said for it.' She soon found work as 'publisher's editor, reader and stooge' with the small firm of Derek Verscholye, based in St James's, and tried to get her life back onto an even keel. Her job was not particularly demanding, giving her scope to dream up projects of her own, and soon she wrote to Edmund to sound him out:

> I want to edit an anthology of The Roaring Twenties (to be followed by The Pink Thirties and the Bloody Forties, or whatever they were). Oddly enough this does not seem to have been done here, and I think there is a nostalgia now for those days of insouciance and parties, of which one can see the expression e.g. in the recent revival of Scott Fitzgerald in the States. [...] The emphasis should always be on the theme, which is roughly, <u>Avant moi le deluge.</u>

She wanted Edmund to write the introduction, 'of a rather serious, sociological nature', but failing that, his advice on the enclosed list of writers to be included. She also entreated him to 'think about possible books for my firm – of high literary merit & also potential best-sellers, I mean both at once' – surely every publisher's almost unattainable dream.

In the end, the anthology project was abandoned – 'the problems involved were too many and too insoluble, by me, anyway' – and life carried on, full of diversions and travels and friends, about which she sent Edmund

Camus

lively dispatches. Lunch with the philosopher Isaiah Berlin, for instance, who was famous for talking at breakneck speed: 'When I said I'd liked his BBC lectures on political phi-losophers he said that if I'd understood them this was a considerable feat of virtuosity, of which few of

Staying with the Camus family in Paris; Mamaine was very fond of twins Jean and Catherine

his listeners had been capable. He did in fact start pretty fast & accelerate to a terrifying speed – he said he felt like an aeroplane that has to keep up so many revolutions to the minute or it will fall to the ground.'

Christmas was spent with friends in Germany, fol-lowed by a week in Paris staying with Camus and Francine, their six-year-old twins Jean and Catherine, and Agathe the cat. Over lunch with friends, they discussed the impossibility for writers of being happily married – the irony cannot have been lost on the assembled company, especially as Mamaine had noted, to her sadness, how Camus 'was always going out on mysterious rendezvous about which he tells F[rancine] nothing, & coming in at various hours of the night'. Camus claimed that 'creation and love come from the same source, so an artist who is obsessed by his work can't also give himself up entirely to love; that is not to say he is incapable of loving, but only a part of his emotions are to spare for it. I said that if I married again I would still like to marry a writer; C agreed in principle, on the grounds that only an artist could really understand & sympathise with one's interests & obsessions, & if one didn't have that in common what would one have?'

Back in London, she and Celia decided to learn Ancient Greek together, trekking out to the suburbs to take lessons with 'a charming, very ancient, toothless, bewigged schoolmaster', and were soon embarking on their first translations of Homer. Edmund obviously wondered what had prompted this new undertaking, to be told with indignation, 'I have not got a classical beau and my studies of Greek are disinterested.' Simply, they loved it: the tortuous difficulty of mastering a new alphabet and almost unregulated syntax only added to the fun. Celia continued reading Greek for the rest of her life, settling on the sofa after lunch with her well-thumbed Liddell and Scott dictionary, a small notebook for new vocabulary, and whatever play or history she was working her way through at the time; she was passionate enough about it to select for me a school where Greek was taught over all other considerations.

As her involvement with Jeremy deepened, Celia was ever more aware that she couldn't have the future she longed for with him at that point in his life. They briefly separated, but both were so wretched apart that they got back together again: better to live with bittersweet compromise than to squander the present for an unknowable future? The strain of walking such an emotional highwire between happiness and despair began to take its toll on Celia's well-being, and she again succumbed to illness. It caused Jeremy and Mamaine much joint anguish and they became conspirators in caring for her. But as long

Celia

as she was caught in the insoluble bind of not being able to make a future with the man she loved, what real hope could there be of recovery? It was an echo of Mamaine's dilemma with Camus, and both situations were unresolvable without causing more collateral damage than either twin was capable of.

Eventually, mustering every ounce of willpower at her disposal, Celia made the final break from Jeremy, and set about refashioning her life without him at its centre. She saw no alternative and, although her resolve was complicated by the fact that they lived in the same city and occupied overlapping social circles, they agreed to avoid meeting, to spare one another's feelings. Mamaine's proximity made this separation just bearable, and Celia's many friends and busy job at *History Today,* her rigorous piano practice and the twins' mutual struggles with Greek, all provided daily diversions. But though friends and admirers hovered in the wings, ready to whisk her off to the Café

Royal, the Savoy Grill or a Cambridge May Ball to while away the evenings in gossip and laughter, her heart quietly ached.

Mamaine's relationship with Camus had levelled out by this time to an affectionate correspondence, each sending the other books and records they loved and knew the other would appreciate – a Mozart quintet here, a book on Piero della Francesca there. They shared their existential dilemmas about where and how best to live with complete frankness, for little was unknown to them about the other, and both were by now reconciled to their lives apart. Camus knew of Mamaine's deep affection for Francine, whose intractable depression was now his chief concern, but he was also alert to Mamaine's own frailty and urged her, ever his 'chère Twinkie', to focus above all on her own health and happiness.

In London, Mamaine was being courted by the unlikely figure of Sidney Bernstein, just returned from five years in Hollywood and divorced from his first wife. A dashing and genial character with strong left-wing convictions, he had worked as Films Advisor to the Ministry of Information during the war, where he had overseen the making of a number of patriotic films such as Noël Coward's *In Which We Serve* (1942). Towards the end of the war he had collaborated with Alfred Hitchcock to oversee the filming by US and British Army cameramen of the newly liberated Nazi concentration camps for a projected documentary, but the Foreign Office deemed the footage too inflammatory to go ahead, lest it should further ratchet up tensions with Germany. (The tape – all 800,000 feet of it – found its way into the archives of the Imperial War Museum and eventually became the subject of the 2014 documentary *Night Will Fall*.) The planned commentary was written by Dick Crossman, the mutual acquaintance who introduced Mamaine to Bernstein.

Bernstein, ever the impresario, was in 1953 on the brink of launching Granada Television, which would start broadcasting from his purpose-built Granada Studios in Manchester in 1956; works from his impressive art collection adorned the Studio's walls. He was a charming, cultured and cosmopolitan figure whose political convictions certainly overlapped with hers, and Mamaine briefly became engaged to him, but broke it off when she began to suspect that their superficial attraction and enjoyment of one another's company might, in the end, mask a deeper incompatibility. And there is no doubt that she still loved Arthur, and found life without him, if more equable, nevertheless lacking a certain zest which no one else, not even the debonair Bernstein, quite supplied.

The twins still thought of themselves as country girls at heart; nevertheless, Mamaine found much to love about London, especially as it slowly unfurled from its winter dormancy into spring, and the squares and gardens filled with filigree blossom, spring bulbs and birdsong. She tried to entice Edmund and Elena – 'that rare spirit' of whom she was genuinely fond – over for the coronation in May of 1953: 'London looks simply extraordinary, the parks concealed behind huge stands, the lampposts all painted different strange colours. The horses are being rehearsed to the sound of brass bands to get them used to the noise.'

•

Early in 1954 Celia's fortunes abruptly changed with the arrival back in London of her former admirer Arthur Goodman, now a diplomat. He returned to London from Tokyo, where he had served four years as First Secretary at the British Embassy, and he appeared not just older and wiser but subtly altered by his very mixed fortunes since they had last met. He had married Sofia (always called Nicolene) Badeni in 1947 and, a couple of years later, accepted the diplomatic posting to Japan as a way of reconciling himself to the horrors of his wartime imprisonment at the hands of the Japanese. He had a strong Catholic faith and realised that he needed to confront his demons head-on if he was to overcome them and that this unlikely posting would be the best, or only, way of doing so. The couple made their way out to Tokyo, scooping up, en route, Nicolene's son Louis from her first marriage to Count Wladyslaw Bavarowski, who had perished in Auschwitz in 1942.

Louis had been born in 1940 in Budapest, where the Badenis had abruptly fled after the Russians invaded Lwow, then capital of Galicia in Eastern Poland (now western Ukraine), and overran the family's extensive estates further south. Nicolene had left her newborn son in the arms of her lady's maid Aitchka and made for the Middle East, where she joined the Polish Women's Auxiliary Services and drove ambulances in Iraq, Palestine, Egypt and Italy for the duration of the war. Louis was brought up by Aitchka in war-torn Budapest; his grandmother had died in late 1941 and his grandfather, the distinguished and elderly

Count Stefan Badeni, was captured by the Nazis and sent to Mauthausen concentration camp, which he narrowly survived against all the odds. Nicolene, who had come to London in 1946 to study at the Courtauld Institute, had not seen Louis or Aitchka since 1940, and it took some time for her to locate them after the war – they were finally reunited in 1949.

In marrying Nicolene, Arthur had thereby acquired not just a new wife but a traumatised young stepson and his Polish nanny, neither of whom could speak a word of English. They were whisked off to the British Embassy in Tokyo, which must have been an acute culture shock, overlaid onto Louis's challenging emotional adjustment to a mother and stepfather who were both complete strangers to him. Aitchka, however, was overjoyed at the reunion: she had been born and brought up on the Badeni estate in Galicia and was devoted to Nicolene (and indeed the whole Badeni family), watching her grow from a high-spirited girl into a flaming beauty of a woman, talented, bold and fearless – if not particularly maternal, as her quick-fire decision to abandon her family to take part in the war effort had shown. Aitchka took to Arthur Goodman with the same utter devotion she felt towards Nicolene: any husband of hers could simply do no wrong. They made a curious family but a family nevertheless, and in 1949 Arthur and Nicolene had a baby daughter whom they named Cecilia, a reminder of the Celia Paget in London to whom Arthur had been so attached. Nicolene was perfectly happy with that choice, liking the name herself.

The couple led a lively diplomatic life in Tokyo, and Arthur, who by now spoke reasonable Japanese, immersed himself in the local culture in a conscious effort to bury his memories of imprisonment, which he largely succeeded in doing. His love of fishing won him friends beyond the embassy walls, and he became interested in Japanese ceramics and ceremonies; when he returned to England he brought a selection of beautiful bowls and objects back with him. Nicolene was, in the words of a contemporary there, the poet G. S. Fraser, 'extraordinary, like some exotic bird, with a film-starish glamour, beautiful clothes, a pale skin, yellowish-gold hair and a foreign accent. She had a genuine passion for the arts, especially poetry, and wrote poems herself. She didn't give a damn about rules and protocol and gave the impression of being detached from embassy life, even rather disdainful of it . . .'[43]

No more maternal with Cecilia than she had been with Louis, Nicolene entrusted her new infant to the care of a Japanese nanny who taught her her first words in Japanese, and as soon as she was out of baby clothes dressed her in tiny kimonos; Louis was enrolled in an international school. Then tragedy struck: Nicolene blacked out in her bath from undiagnosed diabetes and lay comatose in the fast-cooling water until her discovery some hours later, by which time pneumonia had set in. For a week she

Arthur Goodman

hovered feverishly between life and death, but ultimately succumbed. Arthur, devastated, was left a widower after only four years of marriage.

He was overwhelmed in the ensuing months by the kindness of strangers, as well as of his colleagues at the embassy; people took him fishing, invited him to their houses, did all they could to ease his mourning and this, more than anything, reconciled him to the essential humanity of the Japanese and blunted the most bitter of his memories. But he felt bereft in Tokyo without Nicolene and resolved to return, with his entourage of Aitchka, Louis and little Cecilia, to Britain, to be closer to family and old friends and to embark on the next stage of his career. They arrived in wintry London in late 1953, a curious, disoriented and polyglot troupe of four.

Arthur lost no time in looking up Celia, and they resumed their former friendship: both had recently experienced profound love and loss in their different ways, and they found a deep bond of empathy and attraction. Arthur was lonely in London, and struggling with his oddball family, who spoke in fractured tongues and were strangers not just to England but to English food, weather and ways. Celia had done her utmost to put her feelings for Jeremy into cold storage, and found Arthur suddenly the most desirable man in the world. Suspecting that he might not dare risk proposing and being rebuffed a second time, she seized the initiative and posed the question, much to his surprise: 'Why yes, Celia, I think I should probably love to!' was his somewhat startled reply.

Everyone seemed delighted, none more so than Mamaine. Ging-Ging and 'the fam' had almost given up all hope (Celia was thirty-seven), but here was a charm-ing, eligible, presentable diplomat – albeit with a ready-made family – who would no doubt make Celia happy: there was universal rejoicing. Her friends had always liked and respected Arthur, too: an important, if not essential, consideration. There seemed no point in delaying, so the wedding date was set for late April 1954, and they planned to spend their honeymoon in the south of France, seeing friends including the Camuses in Paris en route.

Given Celia's chronic asthma, and consequent ina-bility to live in any damp or tropical climate, Arthur abruptly resigned from the Foreign Office. Diplomats then had little or no choice in their postings, and he was likely to be sent back to the Far East given his familiarity with the region.

Celia was dismayed that he had not consulted her, as she knew how much the diplomatic life suited him, but he was certain he had made the right decision. They both wanted to live in the countryside with their growing family and the children they hoped to have, and decided to rent a small farm in the Lincolnshire Wolds where Arthur would try his hand at farming. Brave decision: he was already over forty and had, after all, suffered greatly at the hands of the Japanese; farming would prove to be backbreak-ing and physically relentless work. But they found a small farmhouse to rent in the village of Elsham and set about renovating and decorating it with optimism and all the energy they could muster. Celia was entranced by Cecilia, now five, and took her immediately to her heart. While she found the now-teenage Louis difficult and unpredictable, and Aitchka almost impossible to understand (Aitchka only spoke Polish and a smattering of pigeon English picked up at the Embassy in Tokyo), she was undaunted, and only too happy to have embarked on this new adventure in her life.

CHAPTER 16

COLLAPSE

In early March 1954 Mamaine fell ill with a bad cough that developed into acute asthma.

She was admitted to University College Hospital and had to abandon her plan to visit Cabris, a village in the Alpes-Maritimes above Cannes which Camus had described to her often, entreating her to join him there, or to visit on her own to bask in its beauty and peace. It was a favourite place, one that he found profoundly restorative and healing; he always urged her to go there when he suspected she was feeling low. Camus wrote to console her, and to share in her happiness at Celia's marriage plans. She wrote to Edmund, too, but making light of her condition: 'I have an awful feeling I am getting to regard hospitals as [Jean] Genet regards prisons' – she had recently been reading the writings of the ex-jailbird Genet, who glorified criminality, at Edmund's instigation – 'it's rather nice to be waited on hand & foot, to have no responsibilities & plenty of time to read & visits from solicitous friends. If only they weren't always doing extraordinary things to one: I get beaten on the ribs twice a day. This is where George Orwell died – I used to visit him here,' she ends, on a bleaker note.

Mamaine

Two weeks later, she was back in UCH after only a week's respite in the real world, '& hellish as it was the first time, the second was much worse, a real nightmare. I'm on the mend again, but feeling decidedly shattered. Shan't leave again till I'm strong enough for the lightweight championship. In the meantime I'm almost dying of boredom, which is a good sign as it means one is better, but oh the days are so long . . .'

Camus wrote frequently to keep her spirits up, though he could not keep from her his desperate anxiety about Francine, also hospitalised but, in her case, for depression.

He sometimes wrote to Mamaine 'in English, because she asked me to,' he told Celia,

and because nothing amuses her more than my abominable English – and because I wanted to distract her a little from the boredom she told me she suffers from. I am sending her some French books, too, and I hope they will interest her. I am going to write to her to give her a little hope as to my own situation. Embrace her for me, and know that she is very dear to me. Above all, give me news of her. I cannot leave Paris, because of Francine. Otherwise, I would happily pay her a little *visite de voisin*.

'Dear Celia,' he continues, 'how miserable I am about Mamaine's illness! She always seemed to me made for happiness, and for a healthy life [...] but it will get better, I am sure of it, it will turn out well and she will be able to go to Cabris, it is there that I recovered and it is one of the beautiful places of the world [...].'

nrf

23 Avril 1954

Chère Mamaine, chère Twinkie,

Encore un mot pour te dire que je pense
à toi et à tes longues journées d'hôpital.
Courage! courage! courage! le midi
t'attend et les nuits fraîches de Cabris.
Je voudrais bien un mot de ta gentille
main.

Ah! et puis F. va nous permettre le
traitement a l'air de donner des résultats.
Et j'ai maintenant bon espoir.

Dis moi ce dont tu as besoin et surtout
ce dont tu as envie, que je puisse t'en
envoyer de Paris — un merveilleux Paris,
entre parenthèses, avec une lumière fraîche,
innocente, dorée — et qui t'attend aussi.

Donne de bonnes nouvelles à ton
fidèle ("as plants to the moon,
as sun today, as turtle to her mate,
as iron to adamant, as earth to
the centre...")
                    A.

Paris, 43, rue de Beaune — 5, rue Sébastien-Bottin (VIIᵉ)
tu reconnais l'adorable Troïlus et Cressida.

Camus to Mamaine, 23 April 1954 (With permission, © All Rights Reserved.)

How dispiriting, then, for Camus and Edmund to hear only a fortnight later that she was now in another hospital – St Pancras – after being 'most awfully ill and still a bit shaky'. She wrote from a gloomy ward full of patients fading away with dreadful diseases: 'I preferred the other ward, though people were apt to moan and groan at night & utter loud death rattles.' The moment she felt better she was full of hope: 'As I feel like Jonah after he'd come up from the bottom of the mountains & shaken off the weeds that were wrapped around his head, I'm exceedingly cheerful,' she gamely claimed. Her spirits were lowered, however, by receiving the decree nisi for her divorce from Arthur; in her weakened state, this added to a sense of failure and hopelessness that she found hard to evade.

Camus sent her the *Letters of Van Gogh*, which Celia later told him was her favourite book above all others:

> At first she used to read it for half an hour every evening (she was too tired to read much) but she found that it excited her so much that she couldn't sleep, so after that she used to read it in the very early morning (you know that one gets woken up at 6 in hospitals, or in English ones, at any rate) and that half hour was her favourite time of the day.

Only days after her release from St Pancras she had another asthma attack and spent two days unconscious, just three days before Celia and Arthur's hastily convened and twice-postponed wedding which, to her great sadness, she missed. They abandoned their planned honeymoon in France as Mamaine was on a knife-edge, and

Celia desperate with anxiety, unable to be with her as much as she would have liked and paralysed with worry when they were apart. Mamaine was relieved to be back in a private ward in UCH, after her season in hell in St Pancras. Although she missed the interest of being with other patients, she had a steady stream of visitors, Celia, Jeremy Hutchinson, Sonia Orwell and Koestler among them. Arthur's visits made her particularly happy, for they felt as close to one another as they had ever been. All anger spent, only the affection had survived from their turbulent years together; the precious kernel of it all.

Camus wrote on 16 May to reassure her that, with patience, 'all this will be nothing but a bad dream'. He distracted her with news of his new project, a film script which presented him with a completely new medium to master, and with accounts of going to football matches and walking through the hot and stormy summer days in Paris, ending, 'I know you will recover and walk anew in the world.' His letters are drenched in concern for her, and a deep and touching affection. They brightened her days and raised her spirits.

I do not have Mamaine's letters to Camus, only his to her, but her last and lengthy letter to Edmund was written on 26 May, back in UCH, after 'a series of relapses, due to the somewhat elementary knowledge of the effects of this new drug ACTH, which you really have to be careful with or you get a moon face & turn into a man'. She was desperate to connect with the world beyond the hospital walls, eager for news about a mutual friend's book and about Edmund's recent visit to Israel to research his book on the Dead Sea Scrolls. She recalled her very mixed memories of the country but the clear joy of her solitary afternoons in a shady glade, away from the pulsing heat and pressures of Tel Aviv. And she told him of her profound relief that Celia had, in her new husband Arthur, 'an admirable man' to take care of her amid her frantic worry over Mamaine. One can see her tire as her writing becomes smaller and less legible, trailing off into a final farewell.

She evidently had no energy to write to Camus because he sent Celia a hurried note on 30 May:

> Dear Celia,
> Mamaine has not replied to the letter I sent to her at University College Hospital – I am very worried. Could you, without too much trouble, reassure me with a word, however brief?
>> Very affectionately to you both, AC

Two days later Celia sent her reply:

> My dear Albert,
> Mamaine died this morning in hospital after three months' illness. You will understand how I feel: it's as though I had died myself and yet were still alive to suffer. With love, Celia

It's hard to imagine a more tragic message. Celia was in Lincolnshire with her new family that night of 1–2 June, unable to stay in London by Mamaine's bedside indefinitely and putting her trust in the hospital staff to keep Mamaine comfortable and safe. The asthma attack came in the middle of the night, and the available drugs simply no longer worked as she had developed a resistance to them. Her death must have been quick, a seizure leading to heart failure in the early hours of the morning; there was nothing anyone could do.

The cause of death given on her death certificate is: '1. Exhaustion. 2. Status Asthmaticus.' She was worn out by five acute asthma attacks in three months, and three months of fighting back with what strength she could muster; in the end her reserves were exhausted, her tank was empty. Celia had not just the grief but the shock to deal with, the suddenness of it all, the falling away of a part of her that was integral to her being. Her entire life, her very existence, had been braided with Mamaine's like a plait, close-knit, and now that other strand of the braid had been sheared off, leaving her inconsolable. Her bright-eyed focus on her new marriage and family was dimmed, as if a glass had been smeared, darkly: all she could see ahead was a long tunnel of mourning and grief.

A funeral was arranged in Hoxne in the Waveney Valley, Suffolk, where the twins' grandfather had been vicar, but Celia did not attend. She and Mamaine had made a pact that neither would attend the other's funeral: they knew they would simply not be able to bear it. The family were all there, of course, and many desolate friends; sitting apart from them all, cold-shouldered, was Arthur Koestler. He had spent the entire night before sitting over Mamaine's open coffin, and he confessed later to Camus that, 'as those hours of night passed, the horror subsided, or I became reconciled to that new face – so beautiful, smiling a smile reduced to the essentials – that takes the place of the memory of the deceased when she was alive.

[…] All the same the death of a bird, my old friend, is very hard on the rest of us.'[44]

Celia never talked to me of that dark time. I can piece her feelings together from her notes to friends, clear and unsentimental, for she hated self-pity in others and would have reined herself in, whatever she felt. She had her new husband Arthur, 'le roi Arthur' as Camus teasingly called him, to comfort and cradle her as best he could, and she had the overwhelming distractions of her ready-made and demanding family to keep her tethered to daily life. Yet she must have longed to give her emotions full rein. Harking back to the grief she described after their father's death, Mamaine's loss must have left her 'howling in space' again, but a more unfathomable space than ever. If she sought out anyone, it was dear friends who had known and loved Mamaine and with whom she could bring her back to some semblance of life, though talking about her was as painful as not talking about her: with grief and loss of that magnitude there can be scant consolation.

The letters of condolence came pouring in, some entirely inarticulate. On 4 June, Camus sent a note:

Dear Celia,
I am so upset that I don't know how to write to you. Perhaps I will write to you later.
But I am close to you, I share, as you must sense, in your sadness. I embrace you, as I would have embraced her, with all my pain and all my *tendresse*.
Albert

From Jeremy – now perforce on the perimeter of her life –
an outpouring of tenderness: 'My darling, I did love her so
terribly much. She had the same extraordinary quality of
goodness and integrity which you have – and I feel like you
I'm sure in the same way […] We have suffered together so
much, that we cannot give each other any false comfort,
nor can we perhaps expect very much kindness from life.'
He had gone to his windswept and lonely Essex island for
three days on hearing of Mamaine's death:

> It was a strange and wonderful experience I shall
> never forget. I felt bereft of everything except my
> grief and my love – each so intermingled, each so
> tightly bound with you, you who somewhere too
> were feeling the same things – and at times and in
> the end I felt stronger than ever before. I would love
> sometime to talk of all this with you – of the way
> in which whenever I think of Mamaine (which is
> every day) so I think of you, and of us, and so grief
> merges with happiness, and the fact that somehow
> we all shared something so infinitely valuable makes
> her death less impossibly hard to bear.

Arthur Koestler, knowing how devastated his old rival
Camus would be at Mamaine's death, wrote in his halt-
ing French to reassure him that her actual death had been
peaceful, 'with neither anguish nor pain, exhausted and
asleep […]. One hour before her death she regained her
lucidity for a few moments. They asked her, then, if she
wanted them to ring Celia. She replied indignantly that
it wasn't necessary to disturb her; she hadn't any idea that

her condition was so grave and took her leave of life with no anguish, no fear of death.'[45]

Camus replied to say that the past was now of no consequence, and to reassure Arthur of his affection. Also to tell him what Arthur well knew: of his endlessly renewed admiration for Mamaine's gentle courage, her fiery spirit, her very heart. *'Elle partie, le monde est moins propre.'** He reassured Arthur that Mamaine always talked 'marvellously' of him, and that he understood what a great loss Arthur had sustained, despite their separation. He, Camus, had never felt so alone. He appended a couple of lines in French from a poem by Hölderlin, 'To the Fates', which Mamaine had recently quoted in a letter to him: 'One single summer, all-powerful ones / Grant me one single summer.'

It was six weeks before Celia felt able to write properly to Camus to express how important he had been to Mamaine:

> I am profoundly grateful to you for being what you are: someone whom Mamaine could love until the day she died and would never have ceased to love if she had lived to be 90. Your affection and devotion were her greatest happiness, you were such a wonderful friend to her. I know that Mamaine felt, as I do, that love is the one thing which gives life a meaning and makes it worthwhile to have lived. Therefore her relationship with you was extraordinarily important for her inner life, which would have been much poorer without it. I <u>was</u> glad that

---

* 'Without her, the world is less pure.'

16 Juin 1954

Cher Koestler,

Quand j'ai appris la nouvelle par Celia, c'est à toi que, tout de suite, j'ai voulu écrire. Mais j'étais stupéfait et encore maintenant je ne sais ce que j'éprouve. J'ai cette mort en travers de la pensée et tout me gêne, depuis. Ta lettre a desserré un peu le noeud.

Ce qui s'est passé est sans importance maintenant. Il n'y a pas eu de malentendu, finalement, et je t'ai toujours senti le sens d'affection que j'ai senti pour toi le premier jour. Et quand j'ai lu les cinq lignes désespérées de Celia, je me suis d'abord senti près de toi, et d'elle. J'avais oublié la phrase que tu me rappelles. Je l'ai dite, parce que je le sentais, et c'est maintenant qu'il faudrait que j'en sois digne. J'avais pour elle, pour son gentil courage, sa fierté, son coeur, une admiration toujours renouvelée. Elle partie, le monde est moins propre.

Mais tu sais cela mieux que moi et c'est à toi pense que je pense. ~~xxxxxxxxxxxxxxx~~ Elle parlait toujours merveilleusement de toi. Malgré notre séparation, je sais ce que tu viens de perdre. Quand tu passeras à Paris, fais-moi signe. Nous parlerons d'autre chose, mais je voudrais te revoir, je n'ai jamais été aussi seul. Je t'embrasse, avec toute ma tristesse.

Camus

Dans un excès d'amour blessé, ne t'inquiète, elle me disait à propos de Hölderlin : "Mon Zweigen : "un seul été, ô déesse puissante... Accordez-moi un seul été..."

you were so wonderful to her while she was ill, always writing her such sweet letters, which made her very happy, and sending her lovely books to read.

To which Camus replied warmly, telling her how he had been struggling to make sense of Mamaine's loss, that he felt as if his throat had been cut. And how much he admired Mamaine 'as a *réussite* individual* – I loved her heart, her intelligence, her freedom, her courage, her appearance, and I loved the combination of all those traits. Yes, she was made for life, and now I still think of her as *comme la vie*.'† He went on to tell Celia, 'She and I were very similar, despite our differences. And with her, I always felt free (you know how it is difficult to be free, even with those one loves the most). I was free and in consequence it was easier for me to be better with her than I was with others.' Then he turned his focus of attention to Celia and urged her not to despair: 'I'm not forgetting what she told me of you, and that you were the being that she loved most in the world. I know what this loss must represent for you and my heart breaks in thinking about your pain. Dear Celia, you who resemble her so closely, you must turn towards life, which Mamaine so loved, and live again with us.'

He asked Celia for a photograph as a memento, an informal snap of the 'everyday Mamaine' rather than the studio shot she first offered him. She sent several, along with a small Cycladic sculpture that Mamaine had brought back from a holiday in Greece, which Celia knew Camus

---

*   'fulfilled'

†   'like life itself'

would treasure. Thereafter, they corresponded affectionately about one another's lives, travels and plans to meet up: it was as if Camus transferred some of his feelings for Mamaine to Celia, her echo in so many ways.

Celia did slowly turn towards life, as Camus had urged her to do: she had little option, after all. In the summer of Mamaine's death, she visited a few of the twins' closest friends in Europe, then threw herself into her life in Lincolnshire, trying to help Arthur make a go of the farm, and being as loving as she knew how to be towards her stepchildren Cecilia and Louis. It was a tough moment to embark on a new marriage, let alone the challenge of making Arthur's somewhat dislocated family her own, and with her depleted energy I don't know how she managed. But the dark months of winter brought a glimmer of hope and happiness in the discovery that she was pregnant with her first and longed-for child, who would turn out to be me.

News of my eventual birth, in August, was greeted with joy by Camus who sent a small bear and quipped that it 'has persuaded me almost to learn English, to talk with her in due course', though he had changed his mind by the end of the letter, admitting, 'In fact, better teach her French – that would be the more reliable solution', recalling Mamaine's teasing at his appalling grasp of English. When my younger brother, Mark, was born, he again wrote sending his blessings, and the hope that 'history gives him an easier life than you have had. I think of you often, with all my heart, AC.'

Celia's extraordinary resilience had come to her rescue, and she did recover and bloom into newfound happiness in her absorbing family life. Her friendships with the men who had loved Mamaine – Arthur Koestler, Edmund Wilson and Albert Camus – grew, if anything, stronger than when Mamaine was alive. Edmund kept in touch with Celia for the next decade by sending her valentines. When, in autumn 1959, Camus found the house he would finally buy in Lourmarin, the village in the Vaucluse that he had first visited with Mamaine during their heady week in Provence together, he wrote to tell Celia: 'How I would love to show you my house and the lovely countryside that M loved so much and in which she walked at length with me. But I don't lose hope of welcoming you here. You must know that you can come here to relax, alone or with your husband, whenever you want to. The view is easy and peaceful.' It was the last letter he would write to her: the following January, having spent the New Year at Lourmarin with his family, he was killed outright in a car crash at the age of only forty-six.

EPILOGUE

Mamaine's happiness at Celia's marriage was well-founded. The farming experiment foundered within a year, and she and Arthur moved south, settling the family into a delightful, rambling eighteenth-century farmhouse with huge garden, where we all grew up. It was a noisy, lively household and a favourite destination for many weekend guests – among them Inez, whom we adored and always called Zeni, reflecting her zaniness; Sonia Orwell, who would burst in clutching champagne, ever ready for a party; Freddie Ayer, surprisingly ready to be co-opted into our japes and games; Laurie Lee and his beautiful wife Cathy, Laurie bringing his fiddle to play duets with my mother for hours on end, or spinning plates on long sticks for our amusement; and our Uncle Arthur (Koestler) who would enthral us with extraordinary facts about the solar system and challenge us to fiendish games of chess and Chinese chequers, which he naturally always won.

Happy though our childhood was, I could discern even at a young age a poignancy, a hint of sadness, behind Celia's affectionate and smiling presence. She had longed for a family and she loved us all deeply; the household was

My parents

full of laughter at our antics and comical pronouncements, and chatter and music and visitors and warmth. But when she played the piano, when she held me on her lap, when she gazed distracted into the middle distance, I detected a sliver of wistfulness, an unassuageable longing for someone not there, and as I grew older I realised that the focus of her silent yearning was, quite simply, Mamaine.

As I entered my teenage years, Celia would talk to me more about the twins' past together, and gradually Mamaine's character came into focus: her complexity, her vulnerability; her courage and her contradictions. And we saw ever more of Uncle Arthur, by now married to his former secretary Cynthia and considerably mellowed, and living not far away. He was still a forceful character, still passionately engaged with the currents of the time, and author of some twenty-five books and countless essays ranging over an astonishingly wide terrain that included memoir, fiction, history, ideology, consciousness, creativity and coincidence. It was arguably the range and reach of his interests, and his refusal to focus on one discipline, that alienated some in the academic community, but he was irrepressible, and continued to wrestle with new ideas, however controversial, until his death in 1983.

He had spearheaded (with David Astor) the campaign for the abolition of the death penalty for murder, which was finally achieved in 1965, and had founded in 1962 the Koestler Trust, a charity to encourage and reward creativity among prisoners, inspired by memories of his own three periods of incarceration, when lack of any opportunity for self-expression could and often did lead to the 'death of the spirit', as he put it. Sixty years on, Koestler Arts is embedded in the UK justice system as a beacon of positivity and hope for offenders and ex-offenders who have benefited from its support and encouragement – a remarkable legacy.

Warm, ever curious, a *bon viveur*, a brilliant polemicist and conversationalist, Arthur was now as close to Celia as any brother-in-law could be. She bore him no rancour, remembering only that Mamaine had never, even after they parted, ceased to love the better side of him. Arthur and Celia drew me into their once-shared world with endless stories and reminiscences and gossip spun far into the night, and I began to feel an ever-closer affinity with my never-known aunt, so vividly alive still to those who had loved her.

Celia encouraged this identification by subliminally transferring some of Mamaine's mantle to my shoulders. She often assumed that I would react to things as her twin would have done – would like and dislike the same writers, the same music, find similar things amusing – and even confused Mamaine and me in her dreams, she claimed. Mamaine became the shadowy third in our relationship, tantalisingly present in our thoughts yet absent from our lives. Celia's unintentional equation of the two of us was flattering but also constraining, and I fought against it as I was growing into my own determinedly distinctive shoes, bolshily thwarting Celia's expectations even when it meant going against my own deeper instincts. But it did also afford an unusually close, confiding rapport with my mother through the rackety years of adolescence, and on until the day she died.

Celia loved to revisit the twins' past with the many biographers and critics – writing about Koestler, Orwell, Camus, Edmund Wilson, Freddie Ayer, Inez Holden among others – who beat a path to her door. Michael Scammell, in researching Koestler's phenomenally eventful life, concluded that the hero (or heroine) of his book was in fact Mamaine, and built a close friendship with Celia, who in turn continued to correspond with Camus's daughter Catherine to the end of her life.

She had found, in her own marriage and motherhood allied with a lively life of the mind, the future that both twins had longed for and that Mamaine had been cruelly denied. In 1985 she published a selection of Mamaine's letters under the title *Living with Koestler*. In that, and in leaving me all her papers, a treasure trove of the kind mortally endangered by the advent of the digital age, she enabled their past to reach beyond the confines of that talismanic tin trunk into an era that, despite the passing of decades, still contains many echoes of the one chronicled by the twins. Vivacious, gregarious, unafraid and fortunate to live among the intellectual giants of their times, Celia and Mamaine were undoubtedly hard acts to follow, but how lucky I was to have two such bright constellations in my universe.

ACKNOWLEDGEMENTS

My first thanks go to Catherine Camus, who so generously shared with me stories of her father and mother, Albert and Francine Camus, and gave ready permission to quote from her father's writings. Her daughter Elisabeth Maisondieu has continued that spirit of generosity. I'm grateful to Ryan Bloom for his sympathetic collaboration in deciphering and contextualising aspects of Camus's correspondence. Thanks also to Orwell's son Richard Blair, who gave his blessing to quote from Orwell's letters to my mother. This book has been long in gestation, and over the years I've been lucky to have the steady encouragement and support of Michael Scammell, Arthur Koestler's biographer. David Taylor has helped with queries relating to Orwell, and Lesley Hurst has been a fount of knowledge about aspects of Orwell's life and work, as has Darcy Moore. Elizabeth Conquest couldn't have been more generous in sharing her late husband Robert's unpublished memoir with me and filling in gaps in my knowledge.

I'm grateful to Nick Hutchinson for his memories of his father Jeremy's island retreat and allowing me to quote from Jeremy's letters, and to Julie Whitworth for memories

ACKNOWLEDGEMENTS

of her uncle and aunt Bob and Jane Joyce, Mamaine's friends in Trieste. James Le Fanu kindly shared with me his medical knowledge of asthma and its ramifications.

Sincere thanks to my agent Kat Aitken at United Agents for her faith in this project and care in bringing it to fruition, and to the entire team at Duckworth in the UK, the book's first publisher. My gratitude also to Lucy Scholes and everyone at McNally Editions for the American edition you hold in your hands.

All quotations by Albert Camus are reproduced by kind permission of the Camus estate, all rights reserved. For permission to reproduce writings by Arthur Koestler and Sacheverell Sitwell, thanks to Peters, Fraser and Dunlop; for Simone de Beavoir, the Rosica Colin Agency.

I have had valuable feedback on chapters of the book from Anne Chisholm, Henrietta Heald and Jonathan Keates, all of them acute and perceptive critics whose advice has certainly enhanced the end result. And John Howkins has been sounding board, critic, champion and unending source of support; the book is dedicated with undying love to him and to my brother Mark.

272

ILLUSTRATION CREDITS

p. viii: Mamaine and Celia photographed by Norman Parkinson as 'The "Who's Who?" Pagets' in October 1935. © Norman Parkinson.

p.17: Ibstock Place in the 1930s.

p.20: A 1930s period piece. © Yvonde Portrait Archive/ILN/Mary Evans Picture Library.

p.26: Presentation at Court. © Illustrated London News Ltd/Mary Evans Picture Library.

p.47: The 'Twinnies' and their Twin Apartments. © Illustrated London News Ltd/Mary Evans Picture Library.

p.66: Koestler handcuffed in Spain in 1937. Photo by Joaquin Vazquez Torres, the officer who tied Koestler's wrists.

p.77: Edmund Wilson. Edmund Wilson Papers. © Yale Collection of American Literature, Beinecke Rare Book and Manuscript Library.

p.79: Mamaine Paget. Edmund Wilson Papers. © Yale Collection of American Literature, Beinecke Rare Book and Manuscript Library.

p.92: Orwell with Richard, by Vernon Richards. Reproduced by kind permission of Ben Ward.

p.134: The Schéherazade Nightclub. © Mary Evans Picture Library.

p.176: I Tatti. Courtesy Harvard University Center for Italian Renaissance Studies, courtesy of the President and Fellows of Harvard College.

p.207: Menu for Orwell's wedding lunch at the Ritz. Reproduced by kind permission of Special Collections, Leeds University Library, BC MS 20c Senhouse.

ILLUSTRATION CREDITS

p.218: Mamaine and Arthur shortly before their marriage. Photo by
     Dmitri Kessel/Life © Time Inc 1949.
p.224: Arthur at the Congress for Cultural Freedom. © Photo
     Süddeutsche Zeitung.
pp.234, 253, 261: Manuscript and letters by Camus, reproduced by
     kind permission of Catherine Camus © All rights reserved.

NOTES

Chapter 1: Gemini

1 Eden, Emily, *Up the Country: Letters from India*. Republished edition, Virago, 1983.

Chapter 3: Society and Its Discontents

2 'The Perfect Garden Party'. *Chichester Observer*, 17 July 1935.
3 Mitford, Jessica, *Hons and Rebels*. Gollancz, 1960. p.78.
4 Wyndham, Francis, 'The Half Brother' in *Mrs Henderson, and Other Stories*. Jonathan Cape, 1985, p.38.
5 Wyndham, Richard. Letter to Iris Bennett. Wyndham Papers (Joan Wyndham) quoted in Caroline Dakers, *Clouds: The Biography of a Country House*, Yale University Press, 1993, p.214.
6 Connolly, Cyril. quoted in Jeremy Lewis, *Cyril Connolly: A Life*, Jonathan Cape, 1997, p.416.
7 Wyndham, Richard, *South-Eastern Survey*. Batsford, 1940, p.2.

Chapter 4: Freedom

8 Perényi, Eleanor, *More Was Lost,* New York Review Books, 2016, pp.162–5.
9 'Took the War to Part Them'. *Weekly Dispatch,* 14 January 1940.

NOTES

Chapter 5: A Chequered Affair

10   Eden, Anthony, United Nations Declaration, 17 December 1942.
      Hansard, vol.358, col.2083.

Chapter 6: The Rival

11   Wilson, Edmund, *Europe without Baedeker*. Secker & Warburg,
      1948, p.123.
12   Myers, Jeffrey, *Edmund Wilson*. Constable, 1995, p.281.

Chapter 7: The Affection You Can Feel for a Stranger

13   Quoted in Scammell, Michael, *Koestler: The Indispensable
      Intellectual*. Faber & Faber, 2009, p.246.
14   Orwell, George, Papers Relating to the League for the Dignity
      and Rights of Man (copies). N.p., 1946. Print. UCL archives.
15   Paget, Celia, Interview with John Pickford for the BBC World
      Service, 2 November 1983.

Chapter 8: Hill Life

16   Michael ('Misi') Polanyi was Professor of Physical Chemistry at
      Manchester University.
17   The philosopher Rupert Crawshaw-Williams and his wife
      Elizabeth lived on the Portmeirion estate nearby.

Chapter 9: Rapture

18   de Beauvoir, Simone, *Force of Circumstance*. Translated by
      Richard Howard, Penguin, 1968, pp.117–18.
19   de Beauvoir, *Force of Circumstance,* p.119.f.

Chapter 10: To Paris and Back

20   Rogers, Ben, *A. J. Ayer: A Life*. Chatto & Windus, 1999, p.201.

21 Richard Blair did indeed attend agricultural college before joining farm machinery manufacturer Massey Ferguson, where he
worked for many years.

22 de Beauvoir, Simone, *Beloved Chicago Man: Letters to Nelson
Algren 1947–64*. Weidenfeld & Nicolson, 1998, p.71.

23 de Beauvoir, *Beloved Chicago Man*, p.75.

24 de Beauvoir, *Beloved Chicago Man*, p.81.

25 Koestler, Arthur, *Insight and Outlook*. Macmillan & Co., 1949,
p.380.

Chapter 12: The Promised Land

26 Fleming, Ian, 'Major Richard Wyndham, M.C.'. *The Times*,
23 May 1948.

27 Koestler, Arthur, 'Israel: First Impressions'. *Manchester Guardian*,
16 June 1948.

Chapter 13: Cold War

28 *History Notes: IRD, Origins and Establishment of the Foreign Office
Information Research Department 1946–48,* Historians LRD,
No.9, August 1995.

29 Lashmar, Paul, and James Oliver, *Britain's Secret Propaganda
War*. Sutton Publishing, 1998, p.25.

30 Quoted in Stonor Saunders, Frances, *Who Paid the Piper?*.
Granta, 1999, p.58.

31 Conquest, Robert. Unpublished memoirs.

32 Conquest, Robert. Letter to the author. Undated.

33 Garton Ash, Timothy, 'Orwell's Last Secret?'. *Guardian Saturday
Review*, 21 June 2003.

34 Paget, Celia, Interview with Caroline Davies. *Daily Telegraph,*
13 July 1996.

35 Quoted in *The Complete Works of George Orwell*. Ed. Peter
Davison, Vol. XX, Secker & Warburg, 1998, p.329.

36 Koestler, Arthur, in his posthumous appraisal of Orwell in the
Observer, 29 January, 1950.

NOTES

Chapter 14: Verte Rive

37 Weidenfeld, George, *Remembering My Good Friends*. HarperCollins, 1995.
38 Levin, Bernard, 'Encountering Ghosts in Berlin'. *The Times*, 15 October 1992.
39 Scammell, *Koestler*, p.368.

Chapter 15: New Beginnings

40 Hutchinson, Nicholas. Letter to the author, undated.
41 Camus, Albert. 'Summer' in *The Myth of Sisyphus*. Translation by Justin O'Brien. Hamish Hamilton, 1955.
42 Camus, *The Myth of Sisyphus*, p.159.
43 Fraser, G. S., quoted by Louis Bawarowski in unpublished memoirs.

Chapter 16: Collapse

44 Koestler, Arthur to Albert Camus. Undated letter (in French), June 1954.
45 Ibid.

INDEX

Page numbers in italic indicate a photograph.

McNally Editions reissues books that are not widely known but have stood the test of time, that remain as singular and engaging as when they were written. Available in the US wherever books are sold or by subscription from mcnallyeditions.com.